*Learning and Perceptuo-motor
Disabilities in Children*

Learning and Perceptuo-motor Disabilities in Children

K. WEDELL

University of Birmingham

JOHN WILEY & SONS
London · New York · Sydney · Toronto

Library of Congress catalog card number 72-8617

ISBN 0 471 92442 3

Made and printed in Great Britain by
The Garden City Press Limited,
Letchworth, Hertfordshire SG6 1JS

Preface

The question 'why?' is increasingly being asked in special education. Educators and others concerned are no longer satisfied with finding *that* children are failing in school or in their social and intellectual development. They are wanting to know *why* children fail. The idea of 'specific learning disabilities' is one of the outcomes of the search for the origins of children's educational failure, a search that is seen as a necessary prerequisite for effective remediation.

Perceptuo-motor disabilities have come to be regarded as one of the main categories of specific learning disability in children. Many tests have been constructed to identify them, and innumerable programmes produced to remedy them. Schools and special units have been set up to serve children in whom these disabilities have been assessed. It seems an appropriate time to try to stand back and take stock of present thinking and practice. The literature on the topic is considerable, and even a cursory look reveals the disagreement about what perceptuo-motor disabilities are, what effect they have, and whether and how they should be dealt with.

Two developments make such a stocktaking opportune. In recent years, interest in child development has revived among psychologists, but the focus of research has changed from descriptions of the course of child development to investigations of the processes underlying it. As yet, this psychological research has run parallel to educational research, but the common interest in the causes of behaviour and performance has begun to make the findings in one field highlight some of those in the other.

The second development is the current increase in studies evaluating the effectiveness of educational programmes. Economic stringencies are exposing educational practices to tests of their efficacy and this has led to a general questioning of educational objectives and their achievement. These questions have been raised in evaluation studies of perceptuo-motor programmes, and the answers have not always been reassuring.

At this point in the study of perceptuo-motor disabilities one is therefore driven back to ask some rather elementary questions. What exactly are perceptuo-motor disabilities? What evidence is there that they handicap the child either in the development of normal behaviour or in making educational progress? Do special educational programmes help the child, and if so, in what way?

The aim of this book has been to explore some of the literature in education, psychology and other relevant areas to discover indications about possible answers to these questions. Many of the ideas raised have emerged from seminars and discussions with teachers, psychologists and others on advanced courses both in England and in North America. Ideas, and even more, the revision of ideas, have also been derived from day-to-day work with children referred for psychological assessment of learning disabilities. To all of them, and also to Dr M. I. Griffiths, Dr C. V. Newman, Mr Brian Roberts and Mr H. J. Wright who read through parts or all of the book, I would like to express my indebtedness. Particular thanks are due to my wife, who, in the interests of the family's sanity, encouraged me to finish this book.

University of Birmingham, 1972.

Contents

CHAPTER 1

Introduction

There is considerable concern at present among educationalists about children with specific learning difficulties: those whose behaviour or performance in school is uneven or inconsistent to an unusual degree. Certain children, who show in many ways that they are able, seem nevertheless, to fail in one or other aspect of their school work. One child may read without difficulty, but be barely able to form his letters in writing. Another has no difficulty with arithmetic but has scarcely started reading. These children are characterized by the discrepancies between the levels of their performance in one or more areas and their performance in the remaining areas of achievement. Other children's performance varies from one time to another. Of these children, the teacher frequently says, 'He can do it, so long as he is not paying attention to everything else at the same time.' At the pre-school stage, there are, for example, children whose language achievement is retarded in comparison to their other abilities.

Attempts have been made to explain these discrepancies in children's performance in a variety of ways. These explanations were based on the assumption that the children's achievement in the majority of areas indicated their level of general ability and that some specific cause was responsible for the discrepant area of low achievement. Emotional stress, for example, arising from a poor relationship with a particular teacher might result in severe anxiety affecting reading. Lack of skilled teaching might cause a specific difficulty with arithmetic. Physical defects, such as a mild spasticity, might lead to poor handwriting. Severe deprivation might cause delay in language development. In the case of many children, it is possible to find evidence of such specific causes to account for their discrepant performance. However, there remain some children who have specific learning difficulties and in whose cases there is no evidence of the types of causes mentioned above. A symptom without a cause is clearly unacceptable and consequently other explanations have been sought. These explanations have been formulated at one or more of three levels. They have been formulated in terms of syndromes of presenting symptoms, in terms of underlying cognitive processes and in terms of underlying organic processes.

Explanations in terms of syndromes of presenting symptoms have sometimes amounted to little more than exercises in classification. For example, the application of the term 'dyslexia' to difficulty in learning to read has, in some uses, implied little more than that a child has reading difficulty without indications of the commonly associated causes.

While the explanation of poor performance by giving it a label is clearly unsatisfactory, some helpful consequences have been claimed. One specialist, whom the author chided for using these labels replied, 'It makes the teachers realize that Johnny is not just lazy.' Presumably, 'laziness' was here used as a term for poor motivation, but few teachers would nowadays regard this as a primary cause of low performance. They would see poor motivation as being itself the effect of other causal factors. One has only to notice some of these children's keenness to learn in their early stages of schooling to realize that poor motivation is not a primary cause. Later on, of course, persistent failure may produce dislike of the affected area of performance, and reluctance to carry it out.

The 'labelling' of children with specific learning difficulties has, admittedly, drawn attention to the fact that there are children who show discrepant levels of performance without a history of the more commonly accepted kinds of cause. Since these causes have often had a stigma attached to them, or have implied dereliction of parental responsibility, the distinctive labelling of these children has made it easier for some parents to accept their learning difficulties. Often this has resulted in the formation of parent pressure groups demanding the provision of appropriate educational facilities, and sometimes these groups have organized themselves to set up their own provision. After an interval of time, this has begun to be followed by legislation for national or local provision. In the United States, for example, an act for the provision of special education for children with specific learning disabilities was passed in 1969.

From an educational point of view, however, the categorization of children according to their presenting problems is very unsatisfactory, since it is well known that a variety of causes may produce apparently identical problems. A child may have difficulty in spelling, for example, because he has poor visual memory, because he cannot remember spelling rules, because he cannot think of what to say and write it down at the same time or because he has difficulty with any combination of these component skills. Anyone trying to help the child needs to know the particular pattern of abilities and disabilities which underly his failure.

Explanations of learning difficulty in terms of underlying organic defects have mainly involved the concept of 'brain injury'. The best known original proposers of this type of explanation were Strauss and his co-workers (1947, 1955). They sought to show that children who showed discrepancies in their levels of performance were brain-injured. The evidence for brain injury was based on the presence of a history of risk or damage to the central nervous system or on concurrent clinical signs. The precedents for this argument were the well-known associations between localized brain injury in adults, and the loss of particular functions such as, for example, speech (aphasia) or the organization of purposive movement (apraxia). It is questionable, however, whether such a parallel can be legitimately drawn. An adult who sustains a brain injury may lose a skill which he has mastered. A child who has a specific learning disability grew up with it. Some account of this criticism has been taken by those who change the prefix 'a' for 'dys' with reference to children's disabilities (such as dysphasia) with the aim of contrasting a partial with a total disability.

A more important objection to describing children with learning disabilities as 'brain-injured' (or terms with similar meaning) is that no one-to-one association has been found between the two. The evidence on this point will be discussed in detail in a later chapter. It is sufficient here to stress that a knowledge of the physical state of an individual enables us to make only very general inferences about what he will and will not be able to do, and these can usually only be stated in terms of probabilities. Children with known brain damage have been found to manifest no learning disabilities for example, (some epileptic children) and the opposite has also been found. In view of this, Strauss was prepared to regard learning disabilities themselves as evidence of brain injury. At this point, however, the argument has turned full circle—as Sarason and Davis (1969) have pointed out. There does not seem much advantage in invoking the concept of 'brain injury' at this point, except as a statement of the belief that, in the absence of evidence of any other causation, the disability must have constitutional origins. Presumably no one would deny that all behaviour is ultimately dependent on the physical integrity of the organism. It is to be hoped that future research will reveal the processes underlying intellectual functioning but, at present, knowledge of this area is very limited. To call a child 'brain-injured' provides practically no clue about how he should be helped.

For the educator, an explanation of specific learning disabilities in terms of the functions underlying the impaired performance shown by the child is likely to be of most help. An attempt can be made to identify the relevant functions from two angles. First, the task on which the child fails can be analysed into some of its component skills. This kind of approach is used in programmed learning and is, of course, used by the teacher who tries to understand what part of his instruction the child has failed to grasp.

Second, reference can be made to psychological analyses of functions such as perception, memory and motor skills. There are relevant findings in the extensive researches on adults and experimental psychologists are increasingly studying the nature of these functions in children. Unfortunately, there is as yet a dearth of research relating these analyses to educational performance. However, the findings from these areas of research form the background against which interest in perceptual and perceptuo-motor deficiencies as causes of learning disability has developed. These deficiencies are seen as affecting the means by which the individual extracts meaning from his environment. The functions which are deficient constitute the individual's 'equipment' for acquiring the information that is the basis for building up his concepts about the world in which he lives and for organizing his motor activity in accordance with his intentions. This book is, therefore, concerned with a very limited functional aspect of the child: an aspect, on the other hand, that is of key importance.

The foregoing discussion suggests that the classification of children with learning disabilities is an exercise of limited value, and that efforts should rather be directed at analysing the nature of the deficiencies which underlie the children's educational and behavioural inadequacies. There is obviously a danger in such an approach, that the view of the child 'as a whole' is obscured. But this is a hazard affecting the beholder rather than the child. It is very much hoped that the focus on perceptuo-motor functions in this book will not limit the reader's view of the wide range of other factors which also determine the child's performance and behaviour. This book's concern is the exploration of the potentially handicapping consequences of perceptuo-motor disabilities, and this clearly does not imply that other influences on the child are not important. Among these, the reader will need particularly to bear in mind motivational factors. All those with experience of handicapped children will know that, in the last resort, what a child *does* achieve will depend on what he *wants* to achieve.

Summary of chapters

Chapter 2 contains a description of the perceptual and perceptuo-motor functions which will be studied and of the terms which will be used to refer to them. The way in which these functions are related to each other is presented in the form of a simple model. While Chapter 2 thus offers a cross-sectional view of these functions, Chapter 3 presents a longitudinal view, by summarizing the course of perceptuo-motor development in the young child.

Without some knowledge of the relevance of perceptual development in the child, it would be hard to appreciate the consequences of perceptual disabilities. The various ways in which a 'disability' can be assessed are discussed in Chapter 4. Research findings on the effect of sensory and motor handicaps on perceptual and perceptuo-motor functions are summarized in Chapter 5, so that the implications of these findings can be borne in mind in Chapters 6 and 7, which deal with the effect of perceptual and perceptuo-motor disabilities on the behavioural and educational adequacy of the child. In these two extended chapters, perceptual and perceptuo-motor disabilities and their treatment are discussed in the framework of the model presented in Chapter 2 and the developmental studies of Chapter 3. In Chapter 8, an attempt is made to summarize the implications of the previous discussion for future practice and research.

Perceptual and Perceptuo-motor Functions

A great deal has been written about perceptuo-motor difficulties in children, but there is little agreement on the use of terminology. This chapter is aimed at identifying the functions involved in perceptuo-motor performance and at explaining the terms which will be used to refer to them in this book.

The confusion about terminology arises from several sources. Concern about children's perceptuo-motor difficulties started, largely independently, among workers with different professional backgrounds, such as education, psychology and medicine. All were concerned to explain the apparently inconsistent behaviour of children, and attempted to do so from their own theoretical standpoints. A second source of confusion is our limited knowledge of the nature of human perceptual processes. While a good deal is known about very specific aspects of perceptual function, more comprehensive accounts still take the form of hypotheses and 'models', each of which tends to be limited to the particular aspects of behaviour in which its proponent is interested.

Within the educational field itself, different uses of terminology have arisen from the particular special educational emphases adopted by educators. Some have been concerned about children's disorganized movements and so have emphasized the motor aspects of children's disabilities. Others have stressed the children's confusion in visual discrimination and so have been interested in visual perception. Others again have been concerned with children's behavioural problems. Cruickshank (1966) cites a study in which thirty-eight terms were found to be used with reference to specific learning disabilities in children.

In view of this confusion about terminology it may be simplest to go back and look at some of the difficulties which children show. We can then try to identify some of the functions involved.

If one asks a teacher in what type of task a child's perceptuo-motor difficulties might be manifested, she frequently refers to poor pattern copying. If one watches the child copying a pattern and looks at his final product, discrepancies between his performance on different aspects of this task become apparent, and provide an indication of the various distinct functions which may underlie the child's performance. The following account of children's attempts to copy patterns is intended to identify some of the component functions of perceptuo-motor performance.

Children were asked to copy the patterns shown in the top row of Figure 2.1. The girl who made the copies in line 2 said, 'Why do you ask me to copy these patterns? You know I can't do it.' In other words, she demonstrated that she was able to see the difference between the patterns she produced, and those she was meant to be copying. At the same time, this discrimination did not enable her to perform the appropriate actions to produce a pattern which would correspond to the one she was trying to copy. This discrepancy between performance on two tasks involving the same pattern suggests that two separate functions are involved. The functions concerned with discrimination will be referred to as *sensory organization* and the functions concerned with making the appropriate actions as *motor organization*.

The pattern copies in line 3 were drawn by a child with an ocular defect (nystagmus). These very satisfactory copies were thus achieved in spite of ocular impairment and indicate that the child's sensory and motor organization were adequate. Sensory organization thus has to be seen as distinct from *receptor efficiency*, the adequacy of the various sense receptors (for example, eyes, ears, etc.).

The pattern copies in line 4 were made by a boy with defective muscular coordination (athetosis). He copied the patterns by building them up with short strokes coinciding with his involuntary movements. The quality of his copies shows that he was still able to organize his movement in spite of the inefficiency of his muscular coordination. The organization of movement thus has to be seen as distinct from *effector efficiency*—the adequacy of reflex and lower-level muscular coordination.

The pattern copies in line 5 were made by an eight-year-old girl who had no defects of receptor or effector efficiency. She had been given the triangular pattern to copy first and she produced the amorphous closed shapes shown for all the line patterns given to her. She was reminded to look carefully at the patterns. When asked whether the copies she had drawn looked like the patterns, she insisted that they did. She changed her copies only when she was given a pattern made up of dots. These she reproduced as amorphous groups of dots. This indicated that she was able to discriminate the patterns presented to her to a certain extent, but that she was distinguishing only between line and dot patterns. In other words, her decision rule appeared to be 'Draw lines for line figures and dots for dot figures'. This girl's pattern copies indicate the contribution of conceptual processes to perceptuo-motor performance and these need to be

Figure 2.1. Pattern copies made by children with different types of handicaps.
(See text)

distinguished from both sensory and motor organization processes. Conceptual processes are clearly only one among many determinants of perceptuo-motor performance, and will be collectively referred to as *decision-making* processes.

This analysis of children's attempts to copy patterns has emphasized discrepancies between different aspects of their performance. These discrepancies have been used as a basis for postulating some of the component functions in the model of perceptuo-motor performance shown in Figure 2.2. Although introduced here in the context of pattern copying, the model is intended to be applicable to the discussion of behavioural and educational adequacy in general.

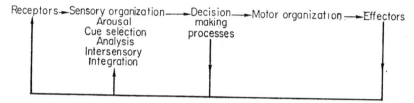

Figure 2.2. Functions relevant to sensory and motor organization

This type of model is in many ways similar to those produced by many other psychologists (Fellows 1968, Morris and Whiting 1971) who have attempted to explain the chain of events in an organism, from the reception of sensory information to action. It is important to emphasize the very limited implications of such a model. First, it serves to provide a conceptual framework for considering only one particular aspect of behaviour, without carrying any implications about other aspects of behaviour not under consideration. Second, as Fellows (1968) points out, such a model is a 'blueprint' for particular functional characteristics and carries no necessary implications about the actual neurophysiological processes which may underlie them.

For our purposes, the model is intended to clarify the various aspects of perceptuo-motor functions that it may prove useful to distinguish and to illustrate some of the ways in which these functions may interact.

Receptor efficiency

A certain level of receptor efficiency is essential for a child to be able to respond. A child who is profoundly deaf will, of course, not respond to sound but, given a lesser degree of deafness, we cannot predict whether or not he will respond. In other words, receptor efficiency is a necessary but not a sufficient condition for a response to occur. This question will be considered further in Chapter 5, but this book is not primarily concerned with defects in receptor efficiency as such.

Sensory organization

The processes included under this heading are those that determine whether and in what way sensation, or receptor activation, is incorporated into experience. Functions associated with the term 'perception' are included in this category, but psychologists differ in their delineation of the functions they subsume under this term. This book will not consider that controversy; readers who are interested to do so are referred to the extensive literature on the topic (for example, Gibson, 1969).

A prime characteristic of sensory organization is its selectivity, or what may be referred to as 'attention'. Jeffrey (1968) subdivides attention into different component functions which include 'arousal' and 'cue selection'. These have been included under 'sensory organization' in the model in Figure 2.2. '*Arousal*' refers to the individual's psychological state, ranging from wakefulness to sleep. Lack of response to stimulation during sleep does not, of course, imply that one's receptor organs cannot function, but rather that one's response to their activation is modified. However, even when awake, one responds selectively to stimulation received from the environment'. *Cue selection* is the term used in the model to refer to this Cue selection takes place at increasing degrees of specificity. For example, the reader of this book will, while he is reading, not be aware of the feel of the clothes on his skin. Similarly, in reading, he is attending to the printed shapes on the paper and not, for example, to the density of the printing ink.

The selected stimulus features have in turn to be *analysed* in order to be experienced as 'units'. For example, the successive notes of a tune are experienced as a tune only to the extent to which they are grouped as a sequence. It is evident that the distinction between cue selection and analysis is rather arbitrary, but the distinction will be seen to be of use in later chapters.

The last function listed under sensory organization is *intersensory integration*. One's environment is experienced through a variety of senses. One hears, sees and smells bacon frying in the pan at one and the same time and the experience of the frying bacon is a combination of these sensations. In the course of the child's development, the sensory qualities of an object become associated, so that one speaks of a chair 'looking' hard and of a steak 'looking' tasty.

Motor organization

The distinction between *effector efficiency* and *motor organization* has already been illustrated in the earlier part of the chapter. This also is a distinction which it is difficult to draw in practice, but which will prove useful in later discussion. Motor organization refers to the individual's capacity to organize his movements according to his intention. The organization of movement appears to take a hierarchical form. In the course of development or in the acquisition of a skill, movements come to be grouped into sequences or into what Connolly (1970) calls 'subroutines' which, in turn, are themselves then organized into sequences. For example, the child who is learning to write forms each letter of a word as a separate unit, but as he progresses, letter groups and then whole words will become the units of movement to be 'organized'.

So far, little has been said about the way in which the functions included in the model interact. Some of this interaction is illustrated by the spatial relationships in which the functions are set out in Figure 2.2, and by the lines drawn between them. Once again, it has to be emphasized that these are only some of the possible interactional features selected as relevant to the present discussion. The interaction can be seen in a short- and in a long-term context. In the short term, the individual can be seen as continually monitoring his own response in the attempt to match his actions to his experience. This again can be illustrated with examples from pattern copying. Figure 2.3 presents the stills from a film of a ten-year-old boy's successive attempts to copy patterns. The first copy of the patterns was made from memory, the second and third were copies straight from the patterns. Watching the boy set about the successive copies revealed how he attended to ever new features of the pattern. For example, he started the second copy by drawing the diagonals, which he had completely omitted from the first copy. He started the third copy by making the outside rectangle even larger, because he had left too little room for the inner rectangle in the second copy. He also was careful to leave more space between the inner ends of the diagonals, which he drew before the inner rectangle itself.

Presumably this cycle of repeated matching, which has been described by many psychologists dealing with perception (for example, Miller *et al.* 1960), also modifies the individual's response to his environment in the long term. For example, the boy in the pattern-copying example above will attend to different features of the pattern on the next occasion and this, in turn, will modify his subsequent response.

These aspects of the interaction between sensory and motor organization processes emphasize its ongoing nature. This point will emerge in later chapters as crucial to the development of these functions.

Several other interactional features of the model need to be briefly mentioned here, but will be dealt with in greater detail in later chapters. It is evident, from the left-to-right arrangement of the component functions of the model, that defects in functions 'higher up' the causal chain potentially affect functions 'lower down' but that the reverse does not apply. For example, defects in the intake of information—in sensory organization

Child's copy from memory

Child's copy from pattern (first attempt)

Child's copy from pattern (second attempt)

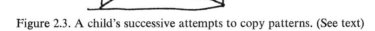

Figure 2.3. A child's successive attempts to copy patterns. (See text)

—are likely to affect decision-making and motor organization functions, but defects in motor organization do not affect sensory organization and decision-making processes. This latter statement clearly needs to be qualified with reference to the points about cyclic interaction mentioned above, but in general it can be said that impaired sensory organization is more likely to deprive the individual of experience and to result, for example, in limited conceptual development. To balance this, on the other hand, it is evident that since the individual experiences his environment through a variety of senses, impairment in the organization of any one form of sensory input is probably compensated by experience derived from other senses.

Decision-making processes

It may seem that elaboration of the *decision-making* component of the model presented in Figure 2.2 has been studiously avoided in the foregoing discussion. To some extent this is the case, since this book is specifically aimed at exploring features of sensory and motor organization. To examine decision-making processes as well would be clearly beyond the scope of this book. However, it will become very evident in the subsequent chapters that one cannot confine concept formation, memory, imagery, motivation and other processes to a neatly labelled 'black box' between stimulus and response. At each stage of the discussion of sensory and motor organization these other processes will be considered as they become relevant.

The terms that will be used in the following discussion of perceptuo-motor development and impairment have now been reviewed. The terms 'sensory organization' and 'motor organization' will be used to refer to the relevant groups of functions set out in the model in Figure 2.2. This was thought to be preferable to claiming yet a further connotation for the terms 'perceptual' and 'perceptuo-motor'. Nonetheless, these terms will be retained in accounts of research where authors have specifically used them.

CHAPTER 3

The Development of Sensory and Motor Organization

In the previous chapter, the component functions of sensory and motor organization of relevance to this book were identified. This chapter considers findings on the development of these functions because their interdependence can be appreciated only in a developmental context. Obviously in one chapter one can do no more than present a selective overview. The content of the chapter has been limited to a consideration of the functions mentioned in the previous chapter. Many of the findings of the studies reported will serve as a basis for discussing the effects of disabilities in sensory and motor organization in the later chapters. One can have little idea of the handicapping effects of these disabilities, unless one knows something of the contribution the functions make to normal development. More comprehensive treatments of the development of sensory and motor organization can be found elsewhere (Cratty 1970, Gibson 1969, Kidd and Rivoire 1966).

In the previous chapter, the interrelatedness of sensory and motor organization functions was stressed. Ideally, an account of their development should reflect this by dealing with all aspects simultaneously, but this would serve to confuse rather than to clarify the subject. This chapter is, therefore, arranged into sections dealing with the development of the individual functions, but it is hoped that the reader will be able to bear in mind the ongoing interaction between them.

Sensory development

In the last resort, the aspects of the environment to which an individual can respond are determined by the nature of his receptor organs. The receptors in the retina of the human eye are sensitive to light waves only within a specific frequency range. The smallest separation of two pin pricks, that can be discerned, is determined by the distribution of sense receptors in the skin. Similar examples can be cited for the other senses.

As far as is known, the major anatomical development of the sense organs is achieved by normal full-term birth. Although the eye increases in size until puberty, and changes in shape, its components are well developed at birth, apart from the fovea. This is the small portion of the retina specialized for fine discrimination, and it achieves development by four to six months (Holt and Reynell 1967). Holt and Reynell state that the auditory receptor mechanisms are well developed at birth, although development of the physiological response to sound continues after this.

An advanced state of anatomical development is a necessary but not a sufficient condition for a normal level of sensory function. Function can be described in terms of absolute and differential sensory thresholds. Absolute thresholds refer to the lowest intensity of stimulation which is perceived, and differential thresholds to the smallest difference in stimulation which can be perceived. The establishment of such thresholds is relatively simple in adults, since they can indicate what they perceive by words or signs. This is less true in children, and certainly not true in the case of helpless newly born infants. Several ingenious methods of inferring whether or not a stimulus has been 'registered' by an infant have been devised. Some of these involve noting changes in the vegetative function of the child (heart and breathing rate), or changes in the rate of the infant's spontaneous activity. Conditioned responses have been used, and also 'receptor-orienting responses' such as eye and head turning (see next section).

Response to sound has been noted in the foetus before birth. Holt and Reynell quote an instance of a lady 'who had to stop attending orchestral concerts during her pregnancy because loud passages produced such distressing activity in her baby'. While there is no doubt that the newly born child—the neonate—can hear, it is as yet uncertain how much he hears. The marked 'startle' response that neonates may make to loud sounds, suggests that their thresholds may be similar to those found at later stages of development.

Responses to tactile stimulation, in the form of gross bodily movements have been obtained before the age of normal full-term birth, in the study of premature babies. Munn (1965) cites findings indicating response to pin pricks in babies a few days old, but not at birth. The difference between these findings may lie in the criteria used to evaluate response. There is agreement that tactile sensitivity is demonstratable shortly after birth.

The extent of the newborn's visual acuity is still uncertain. Dayton et al. (1964) quote several figures from 20/670 to 20/20. Using electrical recordings of the neonate's eye movements in following moving black and white stripes (optokinetic nystagmus) they demonstrated response indicating at least 20/150 vision in children approximately one day old. Clearly such response depends on other conditions being met, such as the optimum distance between the infant's eyes and the display. The infant's power to accommodate (focus) is limited, as is also his conjoint movement of the eyes. Although conjoint fixation and movement of the eyes has been found to occur in the newborn, development occurs throughout the first six months of life. Visual acuity develops throughout the first five years, but the most accelerated development is in the first year or two.

Auditory discrimination has been studied both for timbre (differences in kinds of noise) and for pitch (tones of different frequency). Munn (1965) cites a study showing that newborns under twenty-one days showed differential responses (in terms of activity level changes) to noises ranging from tin cans to tuning forks, in an experiment which tried to control the volume of the sound presented. In another study cited by Munn, infants' sucking responses were conditioned to tones and discrimination was found to improve from intervals of $11\frac{1}{2}$ tones at $2\frac{1}{2}$–$3\frac{1}{2}$ months, to $5\frac{1}{2}$ tones at approximately 4 months. Such an improvement does not necessarily, of course, imply a maturational change.

This small selection of data on absolute and differential sensory thresholds in the newborn provides an indication of the extent to which sensory function is developed at this early stage. More detailed summaries can be found in the references cited.

Development of sensory organization

Cue selection

Given that sensory function at birth is developed to a sufficient extent to mediate some exploration of the infant's environment, what evidence is there of the development of sensory organization?

In the adult a major feature of sensory organization is its selectivity, as was mentioned in Chapter 2. We only attend to certain of the infinite number of stimuli impinging on our sense receptors. Studies of the neonate indicate that he is more likely to fixate some stimuli than others and this is illustrated by the following examples of research on response to visual stimulation. Salapatek (1968) studied eye movements in infants under eight days old by means of infra-red photographs of reflections from the corneas of their eyes. He found that the infants' eye scanning movements were less random when they were presented with a black triangle on a white ground than when they were shown a blank black circular screen. Furthermore, he found that the infants' eyes tended particularly to scan the corners of the triangles. Salapatek considered a number of possible explanations for this selectivity in the newborns' visual attention, including the possibility that they tended to scan contours of brightness contrast. Haith (1966) studied response to a moving light in infants aged between one and four days. He measured differences in the rate at which these infants sucked a dummy (pacifier) while observing either a single stationary light or a sequence of lights turned on to simulate a single moving light. He found that the infants' sucking rate was clearly reduced when they observed the 'moving' light. Fantz (1963) found that infants under five days old fixated patterned discs for longer than plain coloured discs.

It appears that, for the very young infant, certain types of stimulation have greater 'salience' than others. To this extent, the selectivity of the infant's attention appears to be determined by the nature of the stimuli impinging on his receptors.

Sokolov (1963) has referred to some of these selective responses as 'Orienting Reflexes'. Following earlier studies by Pavlov, Sokolov identified certain changes which occurred in response to alteration in stimulation. These changes included reduction in ongoing activity, variations in activity of the autonomic nervous system (for example changes in skin resistance and heart rate), alterations in the pattern of E.E.G. recordings, as well as movements orienting the receptors towards the stimulus (for example turning the eyes to look at something).

Studies of infants of around two months of age have shown that orienting responses tend to decrease when a stimulus is repeated. This has been termed 'habituation', and Jeffrey (1971) argues that this reduction in response can be seen as differing from the effects of adaptation and fatigue. Sokolov (1969) proposes that, with repeated exposure to a given stimulus a 'neural model' of this is formed. As this becomes established, the infant's response decreases. For the purposes of the present discussion, the importance of a decrement in the orienting response lies in the implication that the infant's response is no longer determined only by the nature of the stimulus.

When habituation begins to be found, it can be said that selective attention comes to be determined by the infant as well as by stimulus characteristics. Jeffrey (1968) speculates on the way in which progressive habituation to the various features of a stimulus may result in the infant establishing 'schemata' corresponding to objects. Psychologists have long been occupied with questions such as how the individual learns to appreciate that an object, when viewed from different angles, is in fact the same object. Jeffrey proposes that schemata are built up out of the regularities in the sequence of habituations of orienting responses. His theory also allows for the establishment of schemata of spatial relationships. For example, he suggests that children build up their awareness of depth through the orienting response evoking cue of movement parallax (the contrasting movements of foreground and background when one moves one's head). This point is of interest in view of Bower's (1966) finding that seven- to eight-week old infants already showed constancy for shape (that is they appeared to 'recognize' that a rectangle, when tilted through varying degrees, remained a rectangle). It seems reasonable to suppose that the habituation of orienting responses is essential to the establishment of a child's perception of a stable environment.

Further support for the view that schemata (in one form or another) are built up in very young infants, comes from the finding that if an orienting response to a particular stimulus has become reduced through habituation, a variation in the stimulus will again evoke an orienting response. A study by Cohen et al. (1971) illustrates this. Four-month old infants were given twelve presentations of one of several geometric shapes. This constituted a habituation series, and it was found that male infants habituated more quickly than female infants (that is the duration of their fixations of the patterns decreased more rapidly in the course of the twelve trials). After the habituation trials each infant was shown the same shape but in a different colour, a different shape of the same colour and a different shape in a different colour. He was shown these and the original geometric shape in a random sequence. The results of the experiment indicated that the infants looked longest at the geometric patterns which were most different (that is in colour *and* shape) from the ones to which they had become habituated.

Infants thus appear to attend to stimuli which are novel. Kagan et al. (1966) suggest that infants' attention is attracted by stimuli which are moderately discrepant from those for which they have established schemata, but that infants will show as little response to grossly discrepant stimuli as to familiar ones. Kagan and coworkers based their conclusion on the findings of a study in which they showed four-month old infants three-dimensional models of faces. Some of the faces were incomplete, and others had the eyes, nose, etc., disarranged. It was found that the infants fixated the slightly distorted for longer than either the more distorted or the completed faces. Kagan's hypothesis indicates how infants may increase the complexity of their schemata. He further proposes (Kagan 1969) that at around nine to ten months the infant begins to build up associations and 'hypotheses' around his schemata. The length of time for which an older infant may fixate a stimulus then becomes determined not only by its discrepancy from his existing schemata, but also by the 'richness' of his associations with these schemata.

The various theories outlined above offer interesting interpretations of the data on selective attention in infants. They illustrate how an infant's attention comes to be determined by factors other than the stimulus characteristics which originally evoked his orienting responses. In the course of the young child's further development, other factors begin to contribute to the selectivity of his attention.

Gibson and coworkers (1962) carried out a study which demonstrates the further development of selective attention to specific stimulus dimensions in children. They studied the sequence in which children learned to discriminate different aspects of shapes. They asked children between the ages of four and eight to match a shape with an identical one which was presented amongst other shapes which were varied in systematic ways. These variations included rotating and reversing the shapes, changing straight lines to curves, interrupting lines, and a number of other variations (see Figure 3.1).

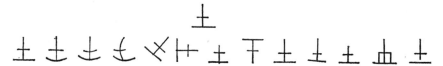

Figure 3.1. An example of the transformations used in E. J. Gibson's study of a visual discrimination task. (From Gibson, E. J. *et al.* (1962), Developmental study of the discrimination of letter-like forms, *J. Comp. & Physiol. Psychol.*, **55**, p. 906. Copyright 1962 by the American Psychological Association and reproduced by permission)

Gibson *et al.* found that, in the age range studied, the main improvement occurred in the discrimination of rotations, of reversals and of 'line to curve' (for example, O to D) transformations. They attributed this to the fact that children were having to acquire these kinds of discrimination in learning to read during this age range.

Maccoby (1967) carried out an extensive series of experiments on selective listening in children aged five to fourteen. Her experiments included, for example, situations where the voices of two speakers saying different things were simultaneously played to a child. Children were previously told which speaker's words they would have to repeat. Maccoby and her co-workers found that children's selective attention in this type of task increased over the age range they studied.

One of the most important determinants of rapid growth of effective cue selection in children is the acquisition of language. For this reason, Luria (1961) refers to language as the 'second signalling system'. Implicit in the development of cue selection is the capacity for abstraction. Language provides an effective means of systematizing such abstractions, at all levels of generalization. No attempt will be made here to go into detail on this extensive topic, but the following experiment described by Luria will illustrate the point. Children aged three to four years were asked to discriminate between three tones of different pitch. The children failed. They were then told a story in which each of the three tones was said to belong respectively to a father, a mother, and a baby bear (according to the pitch of the tone). When the children were retested on the discrimination task in this context, they were found to be able to distinguish the tones. Presumably, by supplying a verbal context for the quality of pitch, the experimenter had enabled the children to attend to the appropriate cues. Such determination of the cue selection may, of course, lead to inappropriate as well as to appropriate discrimination. This is sometimes found in the classroom. For example, where children have done a series of addition sums, they may continue to add when they are subsequently given a set of subtraction sums. Similarly, in a spelling test, children given dictation of a list of numbers may spell the word 'for' as 'four' while those given a list of prepositions may spell it 'for'.

Our analysis of processes involved in perception therefore needs to include explanations of correct as well as incorrect perception. Fortunately, in normal everyday situations, the complexity of experience allows for checking and correcting of perceptual judgments. One of the main ways in which such checking occurs is through the integration of input from different senses, and this is discussed in a later section.

Analysis

An account of the development of cue selection takes one surprisingly far in the study of how the child builds up a stable and meaningful environment. One is still, however, faced with the need to account for the way in which the child's experience comes to be organized into units, or 'wholes'. This problem is an old one, both in philosophy and psychology. Perhaps the only reliable conclusion that one can draw from previous work is that the processes involved must be very complex. Alternatively, it may be that further study of the development of sensory organization will demonstrate that the experience of 'wholes' is an emergent aspect of a variety of other processes involved in sensory organization.

For the purposes of this chapter, it is only necessary to summarize a few relevant descriptive studies. Gibson (1969) cites an experiment carried out by Bower (1966). Infants aged eight to twenty weeks were presented with a disc on which were marked two black circles and a cross. The infants were conditioned to respond to this display. Bower was concerned to discover whether the infants were making their conditioned responses to the display as a whole or to separate parts of it, such as the cross. He therefore presented each of these components of the display to the infants separately. Bower found that the twenty-week-old infants' response to the whole display was much stronger than their response to the separate components. This prepotency of the display as a whole was not found in the younger infants.

Evidence on how children build up 'units' has been sought in the way they use their eyes and hands in looking at and feeling shapes. Zinchenko and Lomov (1960) studied the way in which children moved their hands when trying to recognize a shape by touch, and the way in which children moved their eyes when looking at a shape. They found that there was an increasing tendency up to the age of six for the child's eye and hand movements to follow the contours of the shapes and they suggested that shape perception involved the progressive building up of a 'schema' of the movement involved in the exploration of a shape. Piaget and Inhelder (1956) postulate a similar development in haptic perception, showing that a child learns progressively to relate the respective parts of a shape to one particular 'starting-off' point. They also suggest that this skill continues to improve up to about six years.

Reference to any 'intelligence' or perceptual test (such as Stanford–Binet, Merrill–Palmer, Frostig) shows, however, that children are expected to be able to match quite complicated patterns visually before the age of six. It seems likely that differences in the complexity of the discrimination required of the child need to be taken into consideration. This was shown in a study by Birch and Lefford (1967). They distinguished (among other categories) between discrimination tasks involving the matching and the analysis of shapes. Their matching task involved identifying visually the Seguin form board shapes used in the Merrill–Palmer Scale. Maximum performance on this task was reached before the age of five. Their 'perceptual analysis' task required children to find certain parts of a figure in a complete figure. Achievement on this task developed more slowly; maximal performance was not reached until about eight years of age. Anderson and Leonard (1958) suggest that accuracy of visual discrimination depends on *how much* of a shape needs to be identified in order to make a successful discrimination. They apply this point particularly to shape copying, which will be discussed later in this book. Gibson (1969) reports an eye movement study by Vurpillot which indicated that children between the ages of three and nine become more able to focus on relevant parts of visual displays which they were required to compare.

Intersensory integration

So far, sensory organization has been discussed purely with reference to one form of sensation at a time. Everyday experience is, however, characterized by simultaneous input from a variety of senses as has already been emphasized in the previous chapter. Birch has commented that phylogenetic development is characterized not by an increasing proliferation of senses, but by an increase in the capacity to integrate sensory input. The quest for multisensory input can be seen in the infant. As soon as motor development allows, he attempts to turn his head to a sound source or reaches out to touch what he sees. The use of the various senses in exploratory behaviour has been studied on the supposition that there is a progressive change from dependence on 'near' receptors, such as visceral, taste and touch receptors, to 'far' receptors, such as the eye and ear. However, some of the research cited earlier demonstrates a considerable use of vision in early exploration. Research by Zaporoghets (1965) and Schopler (1964) indicated a trend towards a predominance of vision over touch between the ages of three and nine. It seems that there is not a switch from near to far receptors, but rather a *diminishing dependence* on the near receptors. This is probably the result of accumulated experience, in the course of which nonvisual properties of an object become associated with its visual appearance (for example, a chair 'looks' hard). The predominance of vision is clearly very useful, since it allows the observer to 'take in' his environment without rushing around to touch or even mouth everything, as the two- to three-year-old child will still tend to do. However, when investigating unfamiliar objects, even the older person will still want to touch as well as look.

Birch (1964) has studied the way in which the integration of tactual, kinesthetic (sensation of movement) and visual perception develops. Children were asked to identify visually shapes which were presented tactually and kinesthetically. He also investigated tactile recognition of kinesthetically presented shapes. (The child's finger was traced over a shape and he then had to touch several shapes and say which was the one that had been previously presented. This was done with the child holding his hand under a curtain so that he could not see the shapes.) Birch found progressive improvement between five and eleven years of age. Children improved most rapidly on the visual-tactile task, approaching maximal performance by eight years of age. This developmental trend corresponds to that found by Schopler in the study cited above. Birch and Lefford (1967) found visual kinesthetic integration to be highly correlated with level of free-hand pattern copying in children.

Judgment of space and orientation

The above discussion has illustrated the contribution of sensory organization functions in the development of the child's knowledge of the world around him. He learns, as Piaget has demonstrated, to distinguish between the permanent and impermanent features of his environment, and to distinguish between his environment and himself. This, in turn, leads on to the development of the whole framework of concepts and principles of reasoning which Piaget has identified. This latter topic will not be dealt with here, as this book is concerned primarily with the functions through which sensory information is organized. However, the discussion so far has already demonstrated the interdependence of sensory organization and conceptual development emphasized in the previous chapter. This interdependence is particularly marked in the judgment of spatial location and distance.

Judgment of distance can be inferred in a number of ways. Bower (1966), in another section of his study discussed earlier, conditioned six- to eight-week old infants to turn their heads to look at a 30 mm cube placed at a distance of 1 metre from their eyes. He found that they subsequently responded more frequently to a 30 mm than to a 90 mm cube placed 3 metres away. (The 90 mm cube subtended the same visual angle at a distance of 3 metres as the 30 mm cube at one metre.) In other words, the infant appeared to regard the 30 mm cube as the same even when it was further away and subtended a smaller angle on his retina. Further studies suggested that the infants' judgment was based on movement parallax. Gibson and Walk (1960) came to the same conclusion in their study of six-month-old babies' responses in the 'visual cliff' experiment. These findings suggest that infants at these ages 'allow for' distance in their visual discrimination, rather than that they make discriminatory judgments about distance as such. Size constancy (the tendency to 'allow for' the changes in size of retinal image that an object projects at different distances) has been studied in a variety of situations, and has been found to increase with age up to adulthood (Zeigler and Leibowitz 1957).

It seems evident that very young children and even infants respond to differences in distance in their perceptual judgments. However, some studies indicate that distance judgment develops over a longer period. These studies tend to be those investigating size constancy over greater distances, and those investigating judgment of distance directly.

Localization of the source of a heard sound has been demonstrated by head turning in infants of around five months (Murphy, 1962). Eye and head movements consequent on auditory stimulation have been studied in younger children, but no consistent evidence about localizing accuracy has been obtained. It seems evident that the child's response depends very much on the adequacy of his motor control.

The effect of body position on the judgment of spatial coordinates has been studied by Wapner (1968). He and his associates carried out experiments in which children and adults were seated in tilted chairs and asked to judge the vertical position of an adjustable rod. Boys between six and thirteen years of age tended to judge the rod vertical when it was inclined slightly in the direction of the tilt of their own body, while adults' judgments erred in the opposite direction. Wapner postulated that these results supported his theory that, with increasing age, an individual becomes more able to see his environment as differentiated from himself. An instance of these influences on spatial judgment is given in a study by Ghent (1960) although her study was carried out in a quite different theoretical context. Children aged four and five were asked to judge whether representational and geometrical figures were 'upside down' when they looked at them through their legs. Nine of the ten children studied judged 'upsidedown-ness' in relation to their own head position and not in relation to the environment.

Discrimination of shape orientation is of particular interest because of its relevance to the identification of reversible and rotatable letter shapes such as d, b, q and p. Robinson and Higgins (1967) found that young children aged five to nine had little difficulty in *distinguishing* between pairs of figures in identical and differing orientations, although there was some improvement in this age range. Young children have more frequently been found to have difficulty when they are asked to *match* shapes in different orientation. In this type of task, left-right reversal confusion has been found to persist much longer than up-down (inversion) confusion.

Matching of mirror image shapes was found by Gibson *et al.* (1962) to improve between the ages of four and eight. Contrary to a commonly held view, left-right discrimination of letters has not been found to be associated with children's ability to discriminate the left and right sides of their body (Chapman and Wedell 1972).

Development of motor organization

The development of motor organization is clearly associated with the growth of effector efficiency. Gessell and his associates (1949) have extensively charted the motor development of the infant through the successive stages from lying to running and from gross movements to fine manipulation. The norms of the many infant development scales demonstrate the rapid improvement of manipulatory and locomotor skills. It is not intended to provide details of this development here, beyond drawing attention to the initial fast improvement in gross skills and the more extended development of finer skills. Motor development in middle childhood has been less extensively studied, but Espenschade and Eckert (1967), Cratty (1970) and Keogh (1965) report further developments in hopping, running and throwing skills. The Lincoln Oseretsky scale (Sloan 1955) also traces development in fine manipulatory control, motor speed and a variety of other aspects of coordination up to thirteen years.

Less information is available on the development of everyday skills such as dressing, playing ball games, jumping and climbing, although normative data on some of these are also included in motor development scales (see, for example, Griffiths 1970). Further study of the development of these skills is badly needed. Children's status among their peers depends very much upon their relative achievement in these skills, and parents judge their children on them also. Research is needed not only on *when* children achieve specific levels of performance, but also on *how* such performance is achieved.

Research on this type of question is beginning to be carried out. White (1967) studied the acquisition of accuracy in reaching in infants. He investigated the development of this skill in institutionalized infants. These infants normally spent their time in cribs with screened sides, with little

• •

outside stimulation other than that afforded by feeding and nappy changes. White gave an experimental group of infants extra stimulation consisting of twenty minutes' extra handling each day between the 6th and 36th days of life. Between their 37th and 124th days, the children were placed in a prone position for fifteen minutes after each feeding to encourage more movement. In addition, a toy was hung above each infant's cot. White then compared the development of several aspects of sensory and motor organization in these infants with those of the infants who had not been offered the additional experience. He found that the infants in the stimulated group were able to achieve a level of accuracy in reaching and grasping at $3\frac{1}{2}$ months, which the unstimulated infants did not reach until five months.

Studies such as White's demonstrate how norms of performance can be understood only in terms of the factors underlying their achievement.

Hierarchical character of motor organization

Connolly (1970) is one of several researchers (Kephart 1960, Provins 1967) who have stressed the hierarchical character of motor organization. He illustrates this very vividly in the following extract:

> A short time ago I took my family to lunch in a restaurant, much to the delight of my three-year-old daughter. When we reached the dessert she chose ice cream. There were no problems about transferring the ice cream from a sundae dish to her mouth via a spoon until her attention was caught by something on the other side of the room. As she gazed across the room the spoon, containing ice cream, which had remained poised halfway between the dish and her mouth, slowly turned over. It was from watching this performance that the idea of sub-routines occurred to me. Why could she not maintain a stable control over her arm and hand whilst directing her attention elsewhere? Using an analogy from digital computers we can think of the subunits which go to make up everyday skills as subroutines in a program. The establishment of a fully functioning subroutine would mean that a particular component of a given activity had been mastered. This implies that a child can select the appropriate signal from the array of internal messages. It implies also the existence of an error-detecting and correcting mechanism operating independently for a given sub-skill. In the case of my daughter and her spoon this was not an established subroutine which could be run off; to maintain the ice cream on the spoon required some visual monitoring.

From Connolly, K. (ed.), *Mechanisms of Motor Skill and Development*, Academic Press, 1970, by permission.

In the course of development it seems that 'subroutines', or sequences of movements, become automatic and can become units which are, in turn, organized into further sequences. These may themselves become automatic, and so on. This hierarchical organization of skills is clearly of great use, and enables an individual to do several things at once.

Bruner (1970) reports several experiments on the development of motor organization in infancy. In one study, he investigated infants' ability to grasp a second cube after they had been handed an initial cube. He found that children aged four to five months tended to release their grasp of the first cube when reaching for the second. However, children aged six to eight months were able to retain their grasp of the first cube. This finding illustrates how, already at this stage, 'subroutines' become established whose performance does not depend on the child's full attention.

Lateralization of motor skills

One important aspect of motor organization development is the tendency for certain motor skills to become lateralized. This applies most markedly to manipulative skills. The development of the preferential use of one hand rather than the other has not yet been adequately charted. Some workers have traced handedness back to the most prevalent tonic-neck reflex position of the neonate. However, there are wide individual differences in the rate at which consistent preference for one hand is established, and in some cases, of course, unilateral preference is never established. There is considerable uncertainty also about the relative contribution of genetic and environmental factors in the determination of manual preference. Provins (1967) proposes that, while there may be some genetic determination of the physiological potential for skilled movement in one or other hand (that is, effector efficiency) there is also an increasing tendency for complex skills to be carried out with the same hand. He ascribes this to the progressive transfer, to new tasks, of skills acquired with one particular hand. Rock and Harris (1967) have demonstrated that, in adults, eye-hand coordination learnt with one hand is not necessarily transferred to the other hand. Conventional usage undoubtedly also plays an important part in the choice of hand with which a skill is learnt. Development of lateral preference for one or other foot is also found (for example, in kicking) and is probably accentuated in ways similar to handedness.

Preferential use of the right hand is generally thought to develop in around 95 per cent of the population by adulthood, with a greater incidence in females than in males (Espenschade and Eckert 1967). Hécaen and Ajuriaguerra (1964) made a historical review of estimates of left-handedness. Starting with the estimate of non-right-handedness in males reported in the tribe of Benjamin in the first Book of Judges, they found that incidence figures ranged from 1 to 30 per cent. The greater incidence of left dominance in males is found fairly consistently. Reports of eye dominance incidence also vary widely, from 21 to 30 per cent left eye dominance, and from 1 to 8 per cent indeterminate dominance. Much of this variability can be put down to variations in criteria of assessment.

Spatial organization of movement

One of the most important aspects of the organization of movement lies in the application of spatial coordinates. It is generally postulated (Kephart 1960, Howard and Templeton 1966) that an individual's judgment of spatial direction is based originally on his awareness of the spatial coordinates of his own body—up and down, front and back, left and right. An example of the relation of 'up and down' judgment to the individual's own body was given above in Ghent's (1960) study of children looking at patterns through their legs. Piaget and other writers have shown how, with development, children gradually begin to make spatial judgments in relation to reference points outside themselves. Benton (1959) has shown how children come to be able to copy the arm movements of someone facing them correctly, rather than with mirror movements. (Such development needs, of course, to be distinguished from the ability correctly to apply verbal labels of spatial direction.) Kephart (1960) claims that the child's ability to discriminate left and right on his own body is associated with the establishment of unilateral dominance. There does appear to be some association between these (Benton 1959) but experimental findings have not yet established its exact nature.

One interesting application of the spatial coordinates of the body refers to the 'projection of the body mid-line'. Kephart points out, for example, that a radial arm movement across the body may be described as involving an 'inward' movement towards the mid-line, and an 'outward' movement as the arm moves beyond the projected mid-line. This implies that what appears to constitute a single movement in one direction in fact involves a change of direction with respect to the individual's own body. The effective organization of such a movement would thus involve reference to external space. According to the norms for six- and seven-year-olds in the Purdue Perceptual-Motor Survey, Roach and Kephart (1966) found that children improved in their ability to draw on a blackboard, lines which crossed their projected mid-line.

Children also have to learn to find their way about their house, neighbourhood and school. Keogh and Keogh (1967) have investigated the development of an aspect of the spatial orientation involved in this type of activity. They presented children aged six to nine with simple patterns drawn on cards, and asked them to 'walk the patterns'. They found that performance on their task improved between six and seven years, but that it reached an asymptote by eight years.

Pattern copying

An aspect of sensory and motor organization which has been extensively studied is pattern copying. Developmental norms on copying patterns with bricks or with pencil and paper are available in many 'intelligence' and other tests. Piaget (see Piaget and Inhelder 1956) has traced the spatial characteristics which are mastered by children between the ages of around two to six. Lovell (1959), in a replication study, found that the sequence of some, but not of all stages were confirmed. Birch and Lefford (1967), Frostig (1963) and Wedell (1964) investigated the development of some of the component functions of pattern copying. Birch and Lefford compared the rate of development of eye-hand coordination assessed by tracing and free-hand pattern copying of a diamond in children up to twelve years of age. Frostig's and Wedell's studies included younger children. The data from these studies indicate that eye-hand coordination in pencil and paper tasks improves rapidly in the pre-school years, and then gradually tails off. However, free-hand copying of the same patterns develops more slowly and does not reach the accuracy of tracing even by the age of twelve years (Birch). In copying a pattern with pencil and paper, a child has to observe certain conventions. For example, proportion is regarded as more important than true size. In an attempt to assess a child's capacity to organize movement in space without involving these extra conventions, Wedell (1964) asked children aged $3\frac{3}{4}$, $4\frac{1}{2}$ and $5\frac{1}{4}$ years to copy shapes with plasticine strips. The children were also given the same patterns as a free-hand copying task and as a tracing task. Performance on all three tasks was scored by a method which involved using an epidiascope to project the children's copies on to standard stencils of the patterns. The children's scores were based on the length of outline of their copies which fell outside the stencils. In this way, it was possible to compare the children's accuracy in reproducing the patterns under the three conditions, and Figure 3.2 shows what was

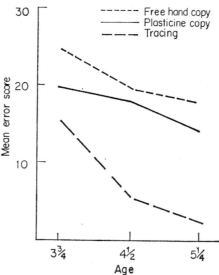

Figure 3.2. Trends in the development of children's tracing and pattern copying. (From Wedell, K. (1964), Some aspects of perceptual-motor development in young children, *Learning problems of the cerebral palsied*, Loring (ed.), by permission of Spastics International Medical Publications)

found. The performance of the children aged $3\frac{3}{4}$ years was clearly still limited by their poor hand-eye coordination as assessed on the tracing task. By $4\frac{1}{2}$, however, this no longer presented a problem. The graph for the free-hand copy scores shows more errors than that for the plasticine copies, although both performances improve in the age range studied. Wedell speculated that the children's performance on the pencil-and-paper task was due partly to the children's difficulty in applying the conventions of copying. The plasticine copying task on the other hand, involved the reproduction of a 'concrete' model with 'concrete' materials, and so was regarded as assessing the children's motor organization more directly.

Relatively little work has been done on pattern copying involving other sensory modalities than vision. Stambak (1951) investigated the copying of rhythmic patterns. She asked children between the ages of six and fifteen to copy rhythms tapped out with a pencil on a table. She found improvement in accuracy up to ten years of age. She compared this developmental trend with that found for rate of tapping itself. She found that the six-year-olds' rate of tapping was already fast and improved little up to ten years.

General comments

This brief review of the development of sensory and motor organization has tried to focus on studies about the nature of these functions. As has already been mentioned, most research on child development has been directed at the norms of performance achieved by children at successive ages, rather than at attempting to find out how such performance has been achieved. Studies of the latter kind are now increasingly being carried out, and this review has attempted to indicate that some of the findings are beginning to link up.

The complexity of the interaction between sensory and motor organization functions has, it is hoped, become evident. The cumulative nature of the interaction has been brought out in the rather speculative account of the relationship between individual differences in infants' habituation rates and their development of schemata. The compensatory nature of inter-action has been illustrated in the effect that language development has on the application of conceptual structures to sensory discrimination. Discussion of the hierarchical aspects of motor organization has brought out the distinctions between 'automatic' and 'monitored' activity.

In the following chapters it will become evident that an appreciation of the complexity of these interactions is the key to understanding how far disabilities in sensory and motor interaction constitute a handicap for the child.

CHAPTER 4

Assessment of Disability

The outline of normal development in the previous chapter shows that the concept of disability, when applied to children, is a relative one. Expected levels of performance vary from age to age and so, correspondingly, do the criteria on which disability can be assessed. In this respect the concept of disability in children can be seen to differ markedly from the concept of disability in adults. Cognitive disabilities in adults, such as aphasia and apraxia resulting from various forms of brain injury, can be evaluated with reference to the individual's language and motor organization before he sustained his injury. In this context disability is measured in terms of drop in performance level. Where there is no information about an adult's performance level before injury, one can at least use the expected minimal levels of normal adult functioning as criteria of assessment.

It is important to bear in mind these differences between the concept of disability in adults and in children. In children one is most commonly dealing with function that has never developed, rather than function which has been reduced. Furthermore, in so far as this discussion is about *specific* sensory and motor organization disabilities, it is concerned with the child who is growing up with functions that are low in one or a few areas in comparison to his function in other areas. Presumably, the performance which a child actually achieves depends on the compensating effects of his *abilities*, as well as the handicapping effects of his *disabilities*. Furthermore, these compensating and handicapping effects will differ with the child's stage of development. On the one hand, specific disabilities may be easy to spot early in development, before a child has learnt to compensate for them with his other abilities. On the other hand, the younger a child is, the less specific are one's expectations of normal achievement, so that discrepancy in performance has to be very marked before it can be recognized as such. It is hardly surprising that a high proportion of children with specific learning disabilities are not spotted until they enter school. It is only at this point that, in a variety of areas, expectations of achievement are more clearly defined. However, by this stage in a child's life, he has usually already had to live with his particular disabilities for five or six years, so that his behaviour and performance constitute the outcome of the interaction of a wide range of factors.

This characteristic interaction of abilities accounts for the fact that it is rare to find total disability in any one area of performance. Failure to stress this point has led to much confusion in the literature. Children's learning difficulties have been described as though they referred to *total* disabilities in one or other area, when in fact the disabilities have only been relative. Reports about reading disability in children, for example, often fail to stress that the failure in performance is only partial. Similarly, children reported as having 'perceptual disabilities' usually manage quite adequately many everyday perceptual discrimination tasks—such as successfully walking through a doorway.

The assessment of disability in children then is difficult because the criteria of assessment vary with age, and because the criteria of expected performance are often not available, particularly in the case of the young child. Furthermore, it is difficult to assess the level of any one function because the particular performance on the basis of which one tries to assess that function is affected by the level of the child's other functions.

'Disability' in the sense of deviant function must, of course, also be distinguished from the way in which 'disability' or 'defect' is used in medicine. Although many of the same problems apply here also, the assessment of organic defect is associated with criteria of disease, malfunction and destruction. It is often difficult to make this distinction clear to parents of children with learning disabilities, who sometimes seem to expect, for example, that all that is required to enable their child to read is some kind of transplant operation or medication. Many of the 'labels' for learning disability mentioned in the first chapter, such as 'brain injury' and terms like 'dyslexia', which sound like diseases, contribute to this confusion.

Assessment of degree of discrepancy of performance is normally made in one of two ways. A child's performance in a particular area may be compared with an aggregate of his performance in a wide variety of areas. 'Mental age', based on a child's total score on a general intelligence test, is the usual way in which such an aggregate is stated (such a total score will, of course, tend to include scores on performance affected by the child's disability). A child's level of performance in one area (the area of his disability) is then contrasted with his 'expected' level of performance, represented by his 'mental age' total score. The degree of impairment is then stated either as a difference in deviation scores (for example, an 'IQ' of 110, compared with a 'perceptual quotient' of 90) or in terms of contrasted developmental 'ages' (for example, a ten-year-old with a 'mental age' of twelve may be described as having a perceptual motor 'age' of eight). The fact that the criterion measures (IQ or mental age) are contaminated by the disability to be assessed is clearly a disadvantage of this approach. Further fundamental criticisms of it are related to (a) the question whether there is really much similarity between the sensory and motor organization of an average eight-year-old and that of a twelve-year-old with the performance level of an eight-year-old, (b) in what senses the IQ or mental age as such as can be regarded as representing an *expected* level of performance. However, these two questions relate to the problem of assessment in general and so will not be pursued here. Detailed discussion of these points can be found, for example, in Cronbach (1960). A second way in which specific disability may be assessed is by contrasting the level of performance in different areas of functioning. A common comparison is that made between a child's scores on the Verbal and Performance subscales of the Wechsler Intelligence Scale for Children (WISC) (Wechsler 1949). This commonly used intelligence test consists of several subtests, grouped into subscales requiring an oral verbal response (Verbal Scale) and those not requiring an oral response (Performance Scale). These two scales have respectively been used by some as measures of language and perceptuo-motor ability. Wechsler designed his scales to yield deviation IQs for each age, with a mean of 100 and a standard deviation of 15. In psychometric terms it is, therefore, possible to contrast a child's deviation from the mean for his age in the ability areas compared. Furthermore, it is possible to estimate the probability with which differences of various magnitudes between verbal and performance IQs might occur. Numerous factorial studies (Cohen 1959, Maxwell 1959) have shown that while the verbal scale may be a fairly representative measure of language skills, only two subtests of the performance scale (the Block Design and Object Assembly subtests) have appreciable loadings on factors related to sensory and motor organization, and certainly little is known about which particular skills are involved in performance on even these subtests. There is little doubt that the performance scale IQ is based on far too heterogeneous a set of tests to justify using it as a measure of sensory and motor organization.

The meaningfulness of discrepant functioning is of necessity dependent on the meaningfulness of the measures used to assess it. In practice, however, it is extremely difficult to devise 'function-pure' tests. Indeed one of the most obvious examples of this difficulty can be found in tests which attempt to measure visual sensory organization. All tests require the testee to make some response, such as copying a pattern, or even just making a movement to point to one pattern among alternatives. However, if the test is intended to measure only sensory organization, this mode of performing the test clearly introduces an irrelevant function. Test constructors have tried to get round this problem by ensuring that the difficulty of indicating a response to a test item is less than the difficulty of the discrimination the item is meant to measure. Until quite recently, however, workers appeared to be quite prepared to regard pattern-copying tests as measures of sensory organization, and this is certainly not a mode of response which can be assumed to be problem-free for the testee as was shown in Chapter 2.

In the last ten years a start has been made in the construction of tests for young children, designed to assess particular aspects of sensory and motor organization. One of the best known of these is probably the Frostig Developmental Test of Visual Perception (Frostig 1966). This pencil-and-paper test aims to measure five aspects of 'perceptual' development: 'eye-motor coordination', 'figure ground', 'constancy of shape', 'position in space', and 'spatial relationships'. It is possible to derive both individual scores for each subtest and a composite deviation score, for children between four and ten years of age. Factor-analytic studies (Corah and Powell 1963, Ward 1970 and Boyd and Randle 1970) have cast doubt on whether all the individual subtests of the Frostig test in fact measure distinct functions. While this test thus provides a measure of a conglomeration of sensory and motor organization functions, it does not yet appear to satisfy our quest for a measure of specific functions.

Few attempts have been made to produce 'function-pure' tests of other aspects of sensory and motor organization. The Illinois Test of Psycholinguistic Abilities (Kirk et al. 1968), as its name implies, has subtests primarily concerned with language. It does, however, include some subtests directed at aspects of sensory and motor organization (for example, a visual memory test). Ayres (1966) describes a battery of tests under development, factor analysis of which indicated that various subgroups of tests assessed specific areas such as 'visual-motor ability', 'interaction of function of the two sides of the body' and 'tactile defensiveness'. Zazzo (1960) includes in his battery a rhythm-copying test devised by Stambak.

There are numerous tests of complex aspects of sensory and motor organization. These range from pencil-and-paper copying tests (such as the Bender Gestalt Test; Koppitz 1964) to motor skills tests (such as the Purdue Perceptual Motor Survey; Roach and Kephart 1966). Many batteries of tests also include subtests of more or less complex aspects of sensory and motor organization—for example, the cube construction subtest of the Nebraska scale (Hiskey 1966). A child's *success* on these types of tests may justify one in inferring the integrity of all the component sensory and motor organization functions necessary for the performance of the tasks involved, but if the child fails, one clearly does not know which or how many functions are deficient. For example, failure on a test such as the Bender gestalt test may be due to at least two aspects of functioning, poor visual discrimination and poor motor organization.

Whether one uses measures of general ability or of some contrasting ability (such as verbal ability) as a criterion for assessing the degree of sensory and motor organization disability, one still has to decide how poor a performance has to be before it is regarded as 'discrepant'. In the absence of intercorrelational data for tests, it is not possible to deal with this question in probabilistic terms. In practice, therefore, one is left with an arbitrary choice of criteria.

However, at this point, a different line of argument needs to be considered. If a decision has been made that the level of a child's sensory and motor organization skills is lower than that in his other abilities, it may still be asked whether this low level of skill represents a handicap to him— whether it prevents him from succeeding on tasks which he is required to perform, or wishes to perform. For example, it would seem likely that the level of skill required to write legibly or lay a table is less than that required to design and make a bookcase. A level of disability which handicapped a child in constructing the bookcase might, therefore, not handicap him in learning to write. Criteria of this type would seem directly relevant to the educator who is trying to help a child. Unfortunately, the assessment of disability in this context (usually referred to as criterion-referenced assessment) is limited in three ways. First, as has already been emphasized, relatively little is known about which particular functions underlie the performance norms in education and general behaviour that are expected of a child of a given age. Second, even where particular functions have been identified as relevant, little is known about the level of function required for a child to achieve the norms. These questions are considered in detail in Chapters 6 and 7. The third problem is more relevant to the present discussion of measurement procedures. Even if the levels of sensory and motor organization required for the various tasks a child is required to perform were known, problems arise in defining the criteria for such levels of proficiency. As Ward (1971) points out, one is even here faced with relatively arbitrary decisions about the specific criterion of performance to apply. Schubert (1965), for example, gave the WISC Block Design subtest to a group of physically handicapped children. He followed this up by giving the children a small amount of practice with the task over a short period, at the end of which he re-administered the test. He found that some children improved their level of performance while others did not. Clearly, the children who did not improve had different educational needs from those who did improve. Yet it would have been impossible to identify these children on the scores they obtained when first given the test. Analogous distinctions are made between children in everyday classroom situations and Schubert's study illustrates the problem of deciding what criteria of performance to adopt. Educational psychologists are adopting 'micro-learning' techniques, of the kind Schubert used, in their assessment of children, since they realize that the results of one-time testing are often ambiguous (Wedell 1970).

This discussion of some of the problems associated with the assessment of specific learning disabilities in general, and of sensory and motor organization disability in particular, has, hopefully, demonstrated the fallibility of assessment procedures available to us. At the present time, when the measurement of abilities sometimes tends to be carried out for its own sake, it seems important to stress the need to be aware of the criteria that are being applied and to ask whether they are relevant to the problem that a child presents.

CHAPTER 5

Sensory, Motor and C.N.S. Defects and Sensory and Motor Organization

Defects in receptor and effector efficiency

The integrity of the child's receptor and effector systems is a necessary but not a sufficient condition for normal response, as was pointed out in Chapter 2. Before embarking on the examination of disabilities of sensory and motor organization in the next chapter, it is appropriate that the possible effects of receptor and effector defects on these functions should be considered.

This chapter will not be concerned with the consequences of very severe defects since these largely preclude function. A totally blind child does not respond to visual stimuli and a totally paralysed child does not move his affected limbs. Lesser degrees of defect do, however, need to be considered both in terms of their direct and their indirect consequences. Direct consequences refer to the immediate limitations on sensory and motor organization, and indirect consequences refer to the effect on these functions of reduced experience.

A further distinction, between constant and variable defects, needs to be drawn, since this influences the child's opportunities for accommodating to the defect.

Receptor defects

Ocular defects. Relatively little research has been carried out to investigate the effects of ocular defects on the development of sensory organization in children. Interest has centred mainly on the possible consequences for children's acquisition of reading. The literature on this has been reviewed by Bond and Tinker (1967). Studies tend to compare the incidence of ocular defects in good and poor readers, rather than the reading achievement of children with and without ocular defects, so that the results are liable to be equivocal. Of the various types of refractive error, the one most commonly associated with reading difficulty is, not surprisingly, long-sightedness. Eames (1964) is reported to have found that *correction* of various forms of anisometropia (conditions causing discrepancies of various kinds in the two retinal images) resulted in reading gain in retarded readers.

Defects of binocular vision associated with lack of fusion of the retinal images (for example, squint) have been found more frequently in poor readers in several studies. Squint is also one of the few ocular defects which have been studied in connection with non-literal tasks. Abercrombie and coworkers (1964) found evidence, in their study of children with a variety of sensory and motor handicaps, that squinting children tended to perform more poorly on a variety of sensory and motor organization tasks. These included subtests of the Frostig Development Test of Visual Perception (Eye-hand Coordination, Figure-ground, Shape Constancy and Spatial Relations) and subtests of the Wechsler Intelligence Scale for Children (Block Design, Coding and Mazes). The children studied by Abercrombie were taken from a school for physically handicapped children, many of whom were diagnosed as cerebral palsied, and might, as the authors point out, have had central nervous system defects in addition to their squints. Haskell and Hughes (1965) studied a group of thirty squinting children attending an eye hospital. Within this group, they compared the performance of children with intermittent (variable) and uniocular (constant) squint on the subtests of the WISC. Children with variable squints performed less well on the performance scale, and this applied particularly to their performance on the Mazes subtests. Haskell and Hughes' results would support the suggestion that variable defects constitute a greater handicap than constant defects but a subsequent study by these authors failed to confirm their previous findings.

I had an opportunity to evaluate the consequences of squint in a boy aged three years ten months, whose condition provided a 'natural' experiment in which it was possible to use the child as his own control. It was possible to observe this boy during a limited period when he had a cyclical squint. This is a rare condition described by de Occampo (1954) in which the patient has a squint every alternate twenty-four hours. This boy's performance was studied on a variety of tasks both on days when he was, and days when he was not squinting. (Practice effect was controlled by alternating the squinting/non-squinting sequence of testing.) Due to complications in fitting the testing periods in with the child's treatment, it was unfortunately only possible to test the child over two squinting/non-squinting cycles, one in each sequence. Table 5.1 shows that he was less able to fuse pictures on a stereoscope on his squinting than on his non-squinting days.

On his squinting days he was slower in completing the Wallin Peg Board B (three trials of placing six square rods into a peg board) and he was less accurate in a tracing task (three items from subtest 1 of the Frostig test,

	First cycle		Second cycle	
Task	Non-squint	Squint	Squint	Non-squint
Stereoscopic vision				
(*Number of trials*)				
Fusion	2	—	—	3
Doubtful	—	1	1	—
No Fusion	2	3	3	1
Wallin Peg Board				
Mean time (in seconds)				
(3 trials)	13·67	18·67	22·33	17·67
Tracing (Length of line				
(in inches) outside tramlines)	5·7	6·2	9·3	4·4

Table 5.1

Findings from a case study of a child with cyclic squint

scored for the total length of line, in inches, outside the tramlines). Both these findings indicate that his eye-hand coordination was impaired on his squinting days. This was illustrated also by an incident which his mother reported. The boy had seen some biscuits on a plate and had said that he wanted a particular one. When the plate was handed to him, he picked up the biscuit next to the one he had named.

Abercrombie *et al.* (1960) suggest that a squint may affect a child's figure-ground discrimination. An attempt was made to check this hypothesis with this little boy. He was given five trials in completing the Seguin form board on each day he was seen. The form board was made of strongly grained wood, so that the recesses into which the pieces had to be placed were difficult to distinguish. White paper insets were put into the recesses for the fourth and fifth trials, so that the effect of the boy's squint on his figure-ground discrimination could be inferred from any change in time taken to perform the task between trials 3 and 4. The boy's time scores were very variable, but the time savings on his squinting days were certainly greater than on his non-squinting days. A more striking finding, however, was that on his squinting days there was a very marked fall-off between his performance on the fifth and on the last trial, which did not occur on his non-squinting days. This seems to suggest increased fatigue effects on squinting days. Some of these indirect effects of squint were also mentioned by his mother, who reported more disturbed behaviour on squinting days. There is some evidence that this was not a *post hoc* explanation on her part in so far as she claimed that the cyclical aspect of the boy's behaviour had originally become apparent to her before the cyclical sequence of squinting.

The circumstances under which this 'natural experiment' had to be carried out, enabled me to collect only very sparse data. The contrasts between performance under squinting and non-squinting conditions were, however, sufficiently consistent to indicate that, at least until the squinting eye is suppressed or corrected, confusion in sensory and motor organization may occur.

The consequences of defects in the voluntary control of eye movements appear to depend on the extent to which a child has learnt to adapt to them. Children with nystagmus (involuntary rhythmic movements of the eyes) do not report seeing a correspondingly shifting environment. Slater (1967) demonstrates the misperception that may, however, occur, when a child is presented with a novel display. He cites the case of a girl with vertical nystagmus, who was asked to copy a capital letter A painted in stripes of different colours. The girl was able to represent the separate colours of the slanting parts of the letter, but the horizontal line was represented by a colour corresponding to the fusion of all the colours in the stripes.

Children with nystagmus are found to be able to learn to read. Poor readers, on the other hand, have often been reported to make erratic eye movements while reading. Bond and Tinker (1967) state the opinion that these movements are the consequence rather than the cause of poor reading, and that they reflect children's uncertainty in tackling words. Backward scanning movements have been found to decrease with improvement in reading. Eye movement studies indicate that the saccadic (to and fro) movements of the eyes in scanning a line of print are too fast to allow the discrimination of individual letters. Periods of fixation between these saccadic movements are reported to contribute approximately 95 per cent of reading time, and it is during these periods that the visual discrimination is likely to occur.

In summary, it is striking to find the degree of adaptation to ocular defects which a child manages to achieve. Little is known about the effect of ocular defects on early sensory and motor organization and about their effect on rate of later learning. In so far as such defects require adaptation, it seems that many tasks are more effortful for children, and the consequent effects, such as fatigue, may themselves constitute a handicap.

Hearing loss. The distinction in Chapter 2 between receptor efficiency and sensory organization defects corresponds approximately to that between 'peripheral' and 'central' hearing loss. However, clinically, such a distinction is very difficult to draw. 'Central' deafness is commonly associated with receptive aphasia or with a more general disability in making sense of sound (auditory agnosia).

This section will be concerned mainly with defects which result in raised thresholds of sensitivity to sound. The direct effects of such hearing loss are familiar. Communication is affected, both through difficulty in hearing what is said, and in the effect of hearing loss on the development of adequate articulation. Most research on the indirect consequences of these defects has, not surprisingly, been concerned with their effect on the acquisition of language skills and on the development of concepts (see, for example, Furth 1966). Relatively little work has been carried out on the consequences for sensory organization as such.

Mangan (1963) reports a study by Myklebust and Brutten (1953) of visual perception in deaf children aged eight to eleven years with 'normal' intelligence and visual acuity. These workers found that the deaf children performed poorly on the marble board test and on a figure-ground test, but not on a pattern-reproduction test and on the Goodenough Draw-a-Man test. Mangan summarizes another study by Larr (1956) who found that younger deaf children were equal or superior to hearing children on the marble board tests, as well as on a picture test and a tactual-motor test. Clearly, this disagreement between findings may well reflect the differences in the selection of subjects. Studies comparing the performance of deaf and hearing children on intelligence tests have generally shown very little difference between the groups' scores on those components of the tests involving visual sensory and motor organization. Myklebust (1964) quotes a study in which the Thurstone Primary Mental Abilities Test was given to deaf and hard-of-hearing children in a day school. Both groups of deaf children achieved slightly above average scores on the 'Space Ability' and 'Perceptual Speed' subtests. Similarly, in a study of deaf children aged twelve to seventeen, cited by Myklebust, the mean Performance Scale Quotients were all around an average level (in contrast to the Verbal Quotients, which were considerably below average).

It seems then that there is no evidence that hearing loss has a detrimental effect on sensory and motor organization involving vision in the types of task studied. However, there appears to be little research on the effect of hearing loss on sensory and motor organization in less formal tasks. One would like to know, for example, how hearing loss affected sensory and motor organization in games activities and in children's ability to orient themselves in space. Myklebust (1954) makes the interesting point that deaf children are more distracted by peripheral visual stimulation, since they are not able to 'monitor' their environment through hearing. (Since hearing is not limited in direction of reception as vision is, the hearing individual can keep some track of what is going on around him without looking.) Furthermore, binaural hearing enables the individual to localize the sources of sounds, and unilateral deafness is likely to constitute a handicap in this respect.

Tactile sensory loss. Loss in tactile sensitivity has been found in children with hemiplegic cerebral palsy (Tizard *et al.* 1954 quoted by Denhoff 1966). Sensory loss can be established in these children, since sensory function on their affected and unaffected sides can be compared. Tizard assessed tactile sensitivity in terms of two-point discrimination thresholds (the distance at which two points of simultaneous tactile stimulation are perceived as separate) and of stereognosis (the discrimination of shape by touch). Tizard and coworkers found that about half of their sample of children showed sensory loss, but they did not find that this was associated with poor performance on block design, picture completion or design copying tests. It is, of course, difficult to distinguish the effects of sensory loss and of other forms of central nervous system dysfunction in these children. Ayres (1965) reported that children with learning difficulty were poor in tactile localization. In a large battery of tests which she gave to a group of children, she included a task in which they were required to identify which parts of their forearms had been touched. Ayres regarded the poor performance of the learning disabled children on this task as an indication of underlying neurological dysfunction, rather than as a direct cause of their learning disabilities.

General comment on the consequences of receptor defects

The consequences of receptor defects have, for the sake of clarity, been discussed in rather unreal isolation. In the real-life situation, as has been noted, the individual is using whatever sensory input is available to him, so that loss in one particular sense modality is compensated by information from the remaining modalities. This is presumably one of the main reasons for the prevalence of adequate performance found in the studies cited above. It has been interesting to note that such compensation has to have time to be established and that effort may be involved in maintaining it. It is important that the more or less normal function found in children with various types of sensory loss should not mislead one on this point.

Defects in effector efficiency

Motor defects also may have more or less direct consequences. At the most direct level, motor defect may preclude a particular type of performance. At a less direct level, motor defect may result in confusing kinesthetic feedback. For example, the spastic child who is trying to judge the weight of an object by lifting it, will not experience constant gravitational pressure due to the clasp-knife nature of the muscular incoordination. A more indirect consequence of motor defect is the limitation it may impose on the individual's range of activity and, consequently, on the variety of experience to which he may be exposed.

The evaluation of effector efficiency itself presents considerable problems.

It can be made with reference to at least three criteria: the number of limbs or body parts affected, the type of neuro-muscular dysfunction (for example, polio, athetosis) or the skills affected (for example, manipulation, walking). In the studies to be reviewed below, the different implications of these ratings should be borne in mind.

One of the main forms of motor defect which has been studied is cerebral palsy. Since this condition is associated with brain injury, it has been necessary to try to distinguish between the consequences of brain injury and of the motor defect as such. Wedell (1960a) used a rating of motor defect devised by F. E. Schonell (1956) which referred to degree of interference with self-help skills and independence. Using a variety of sensory and motor organization tasks with matched samples of athetoid and spastic children aged six to ten, he found positive but nonsignificant correlations with degree of motor handicap. The tasks were designed to be as insensitive as possible to manipulative skill, but the highest, though nonsignificant, correlation between motor defect and test performance was still found in the task that demanded most manipulative skill (a block construction task).

In their study of physically handicapped children, Abercrombie et al. (1964) found some association between degree of motor handicap (assessed on the Pultibec scale) and performance on a variety of sensory and motor organization tasks in children with diplegic and hemiplegic cerebral palsy. However, Abercrombie also found an association between squint in these children and performance on the tasks. Cobrinik (1959) reported a significant association between degree of motor handicap and performance on a figure-ground discrimination task in cerebral palsied children, an association which was independent of scores on an intelligence test. As Abercrombie points out, however, he does not give information on the visual state of these children. Nielsen (1966), in a study of mildly handicapped cerebral palsied children, found a tendency for the less motor handicapped children to perform poorly on her group of perceptuo-motor tasks. Again, however, there was a higher incidence of children with squint among the less handicapped which tended to confound any association which might have existed with motor handicap. The general conclusion drawn by the authors of these studies was that motor handicap appeared to play a lesser role in determining performance on sensory and motor organization tasks than type of brain injury.

The aim in all these studies was, of course, to avoid evaluating the children's performance in a way which would reflect their difficulties in manipulation. The failure to find an association between motor defect and sensory and motor organization may reflect the fact that children with very severe motor defect were excluded from the studies. It may also reflect the crudeness of the motor defect criteria used. On the other hand, it may be that these authors have looked for the consequences of motor defect in the wrong type of task. Pattern copying and matching and other tasks commonly used in these studies require a high involvement of cognitive abilities in the sensory and motor organization required. Performance on these tasks is thus subject to their compensatory effect. It seems more likely that the consequences of motor defect may be found in 'lower-level' sensory and motor organization involved in everyday tasks, such as spatial orientation, distance and movement judgment. Wedell *et al.* (1972) tested this hypothesis in a pilot study on the relationship between size constancy and experience of mobility in cerebral palsied children aged six to nine. Size constancy refers to the individual's tendency to judge the size of an object at a distance in terms of its real size, rather than in terms of its projected size, which is of course proportional to the distance of the object. Zeigler and Leibowitz (1957) found that normal children, as they grew older, tended increasingly to judge the size of a rod placed at a distance according to its real size. These researchers found that the age differences in size constancy became apparent when the rods were placed at more than 10 feet from the children. Wedell *et al.* tested small groups of cerebral palsied children in schools for physically handicapped children and were not able to use distances over 17 feet. Their results provided consistent indications that children who were chair-bound or had begun to walk independently only within the previous eighteen months showed lesser size constancy than children who had walked independently for longer. Differences in age and verbal intelligence among the subjects in this study were controlled. Possible differences between the groups in degree and type of brain injury were, of course, not ruled out. However, no differences in accuracy of judgment were found between the groups, and this would have seemed a measure more likely to reflect any effect of brain injury on the performance of this task. Although this study represents only pilot research, it does indicate that both choice of task and measure of defect may influence whether motor defect is shown to affect sensory and motor organization.

The brief survey of studies in this section indicates that information on the effect of receptor and effector deficiencies on sensory and motor organization has to be derived mainly from studies on other related conditions. The direct effects of the deficiencies are fairly easy to identify, but the indirect effects are less evident. The findings of some of the studies quoted suggest areas where consequences for sensory and motor organization are likely to be found.

Central nervous system defects

Diagnosis of C.N.S. defects in children may be based on a variety of data. The most unequivocal diagnoses are those based on direct observation of, for example, cerebral lesions such as might result from some form of physical insult to the cortex sustained in an accident. More commonly, C.N.S. defect is inferred from the presence of certain well-established clinical signs, such as abnormal reflex responses or E.E.G. records. Often, the presence of C.N.S. defect is inferred from aspects of a child's medical history, such as anoxia at birth, or severe febrile attacks. The above grounds for diagnoses of C.N.S. defects have been listed in increasing degree of conjecture. However, regardless of its reliability, the diagnosis of C.N.S. defect in the majority of instances does not have specific implications for functional loss. In particular, little is yet known about the consequences of C.N.S. defects for children's sensory organization and cognitive processes. This is hardly surprising, as has already been indicated in the first chapter, since both the complexity of these processes as well as the variety of C.N.S. defects is so great. This variety has been excellently described by Birch (1964). It is sufficient here to indicate some distinctions which have been used in relevant research. Studies have been carried out in which disabilities in sensory and motor organization have been related to the amount, 'level' and location of C.N.S. defect, and to the child's stage of development at onset of defect. This discussion will confine itself to studies in which the diagnosis of C.N.S. defect is based either on evidence of specific traumata, or on recognized clinical signs. Innumerable studies have shown that children diagnosed as 'brain injured' are more likely to show impaired sensory and motor organization than children without evidence of brain injury. Wide variations in performance have almost invariably been found in both pathological and control groups, and this has indicated that impairment of sensory and motor organization is probably associated with some particular forms of C.N.S. defect rather than others. Cruickshank et al. (1965) carried out a study comparing the performance of a large group of 114 athetoid and of 211 spastic children on tests of figure-ground discrimination. The children were aged between six and sixteen years and were matched by groups for age and intelligence. The spastic children's performance was consistently lower than that of the athetoids (who, in turn, were slightly poorer than a control group). Since athetosis is associated with damage to the basal ganglia of the midbrain, while spasticity may be associated with damage to the motor cortex, Cruickshank et al.'s study suggested that impairment in figure-ground discrimination was associated with cortical damage.

Nielson (1966) compared the incidence of sensory and motor organization disability in spastic hemiplegic and paraplegic children between six and fifteen years of age. She found impaired performance more frequently among the hemiplegics in her sample, whom she regarded as constituting a more pathological group than her sample of paraplegics. This indication was supported in her study, since half the hemiplegic but none of the paraplegic children had convulsive disorders. Epilepsy as such has not been found to be associated with sensory or motor organization disability, and so Nielsen's finding may indicate that extent of cortical damage is a relevant factor.

Wedell (1960b), in the study mentioned earlier, investigated matched samples of athetoids and of spastics with predominant bilateral, left- and right-sided motor defect. His children were between six and ten years of age, and had measured global IQs between 60 and 120. He found that his combined spastic groups' performance on a variety of sensory and motor organization tasks was lower than that of the athetoids, thus confirming Cruickshank's findings. He also found that the performance of the children with predominant bilateral and left-sided motor defect was worse than that of the group with right-sided motor defect. There was no significant difference between the degree of visual and motor defect of the left and right hemiplegic groups, and the results were taken to indicate an association between some aspects of right-sided brain injury and impairment of sensory and motor organization. Such a hypothesis goes against the generally held assumptions about the plasticity of cortical function in early life. While amount of cortical damage might well affect the scope for the development of sensory and motor organization, injury in one particular area would presumably result in function being taken over by another area. However, Wedell's finding is consistent with the findings for adults and for children with brain injury sustained after the age of one (McFie 1961a and 1961b).

Studies on spastic children have, for the major part, not been directed at systematic comparisons of left and right hemiplegics. Among researchers who did make this comparison, Wood (1955) found no significant differences, and Nielsen (1966) found poorer performance among left hemiplegics. Miscellaneous indications from other studies are not found to support Wedell's findings. In a follow-up study, after about 2½ years, of some of the children in each of his spastic groups, Wedell (1961) found that the difference in the groups' performance levels in sensory and motor organization tasks persisted. However, while seven of the eight right hemiplegics who were followed up had gone on into ordinary schools, this was the case in only four of the eight left hemiplegics. One is then left with the question of whether the groups were in fact dissimilar in the first place, or whether the different school performance reflected the consequences of their poor sensory and motor organization.

The relevance of age at onset of C.N.S. defect for the consequent development of sensory and motor organization has not been extensively researched. McFie (1961a) reported findings on a group of children with various types of brain injury and predominantly below-average scores on intelligence tests.

A verbal-performance test discrepancy in favour of verbal scores occurred more frequently in the group of children who had sustained right-sided brain injury after one year of age. Discrepancies in the opposite direction occurred more frequently in the children injured in either hemisphere before one year. It is not certain, however, what significance can be attached to these findings, since the discrepancies were in some cases inferred from scores on specific items in global intelligence tests. In another study of children with various types of brain injury who were tested between the ages of five and fifteen before being given a hemispherectomy operation, McFie (1961b) found that poor performance on sensory and motor organization tasks (WISC Block Design and Picture Arrangement subtests and Stanford–Binet Memory for Designs) was associated with right cerebral lesions. A further analysis suggested that impairment was specifically associated with injury in the right parietal area. Annette et al. (1961) studied E.E.G. foci in children attending a neuropsychiatric clinic. Many of the children had histories of early brain injury, and over half had sustained their first epileptic attack before the age of four. Examination of the WISC scores of forty of these children revealed that children with E.E.G. foci on the same side as their dominant hand (that is, in the minor hemisphere) tended to have lower scores on the performance scale than on the verbal scale. A discrepancy in the opposite direction was found in children with contralateral foci, and in those with mixed handedness. On the basis of their findings these authors put forward an interesting hypothesis. Emphasizing that sensory and motor organization starts to be developed before language skills, they postulated that the former became established in whichever hemisphere was more intact. When language skills begin to be learnt, these are then subserved by the less intact hemisphere and this results in relative impairment of language development (as McFie (1961a) also found). Annette et al. also postulated that in some children cerebral dominance and hand dominance is strongly genetically determined, and that when this is the case, the minor hemisphere subserves sensory and motor organization regardless of its functional state. They suggest that if the minor hemisphere is then damaged, lower performance than verbal scores will be found.

The authors admit that this is a highly speculative view. It is mentioned here primarily because it emphasizes that the development of sensory and motor organization starts before language development. This has tended to be forgotten in considerations about the consequences of brain injury. These findings and those of McFie also stress that C.N.S. defects may result in language deficiency just as much as in poor sensory and motor organization. Selective impairment, whether of verbal or nonverbal abilities, resulting from brain injury before the first year of life, is incompatible with the generally held views of plasticity of cortical function and requires some explanation. Annette *et al.*'s hypothesis provides a possible account.

Poor sensory and motor organization appears, then, to be associated with cortical lesions. There is some indication that it is associated with minor-hemisphere lesions, but there is more evidence that this trend holds for injuries sustained after the first year of life.

The findings surveyed show that general statements cannot be made about the relationship between C.N.S. defects and disabilities in sensory and motor organization.

CHAPTER 6

Sensory and Motor Organization Disabilities and Behavioural Adequacy

This chapter will be concerned with two main topics: first, the nature of disabilities in sensory and motor organization, and second, an examination of their possible effect on behavioural adequacy in children. 'Behavioural adequacy' is used here as a portmanteau term referring to the efficiency with which a child responds to his social and physical environment in general. The chapter will look at both direct and indirect evidence of behavioural adequacy. Studies offering direct evidence are those describing specific aspects of behaviour such as, for example, distractibility. Studies offering indirect evidence are those comparing sensory and motor organization in groups of deviant children (for example, autistic or brain-injured) children. The evidence on behavioural inadequacy in these groups of deviant children is indirect, in so far as it is inferred from the implications of their diagnostic label. In the case of autistic children, such an inference about behavioural inadequacy is self-evident. In the case of other diagnostic groups, such as brain-injured children, the inference is based on the fact that, in the studies cited, there are implications that the children are showing various forms of behavioural inadequacy.

Only studies that investigate sensory and motor organization functions in children showing behavioural inadequacy will be examined. In view of this, it will, of course, be important for the reader to remember that disabilities in sensory and motor organization are not the only possible causes of the types of behavioural inadequacy described. Furthermore, this survey of research will also illustrate how the effect of disabilities in sensory and motor organization ranges from direct to indirect, as was mentioned in Chapter 3. Once again, the studies cited are almost exclusively concerned with the visual modality.

The sections of the chapter are arranged according to the various component sensory and motor organization functions mentioned in Chapter 2. Findings on the effect of remedial measures will be dealt with in the final section, but they will also be mentioned in the earlier sections if they provide evidence on the relation of sensory and motor organization to behavioural adequacy.

Sensory organization

Deficiencies in the component functions of sensory organization will be considered in turn.

Arousal

The previous chapter dealt with ways in which children's sensitivity was reduced by impairment of their receptor organs. There is evidence that, in some children, response to stimulation varies in other and sometimes paradoxical ways.

Some children have been found to show increased response to stimulation in certain sense modalities. Goldfarb (1964) and Rimland (1964) describe hypersensitivity to loud sounds in autistic children. This hypersensitivity is inferred mainly from the catastrophic responses the child may make to a loud sound. Such responses are familiar in one's experience of these children. For example, a five-year-old 'autistic' boy who attended a weekly playgroup would become terror struck whenever another child fired a cap-pistol in play. He responded in this way even when the pistol was fired in a part of the playroom remote from him, and when he was not himself involved in the game of Cowboys and Indians.

Hermelin and O'Connor (1970) in a study of E.E.G. changes to stimulation, found that, in contrast to a control group, autistic children were more aroused by a continuous sound, but not by a continuous light. These researchers stressed, however, that these differences between autistic and 'normal' children varied with the kind of auditory and visual stimuli used.

Ayres (1965) noted that some of the children in her learning disability group showed hypersensitivity to touch. Here again, the greater sensitivity was inferred from exaggerated response, which she described as 'defensiveness'. Part of her diagnostic and remedial measures involve stroking the child's hand and forearm with a brush, and she found that some children showed marked aversion to this.

Hypersensitivity may, of course, also be attributed to emotionally traumatic experiences and other psychogenic causes. However, the implication in the studies cited is that it may occur as a primary condition. Goldfarb (1964) suggests that hypersensitivity at an early age may contribute to the unresponsiveness shown by autistic children at a later age. Such a hypothesis would offer an explanation for the paradoxical response to sound which one sometimes obtains, where the child turns to a soft but not to a loud sound, or responds after an interval of time.

Luria (1963), in his study of mentally retarded children, explains abnormalities in responsiveness in terms of a generalized disturbance of the balance between the 'excitatory' and 'inhibitory' aspects of neural activity in the cortex. This neurological distinction is primarily inferred from differences he observed in children's response to conditioning.

On the basis of the evidence cited in this section, it appears that differences in response to stimulation have been found among children showing deviant behaviour. It is not clear, however, whether these represent differences in sensitivity, or differences in response to a given level of stimulation. Differences in sensitivity would imply that the child responded, for example, to sounds which were imperceptible to others. Goldfarb (1964), however, found normal visual and auditory acuity among his autistic children. It seems more likely that these children respond in an exaggerated way to stimuli within the normal range of sensitivity. Hutt and Hutt (1970) suggest that autistic children are more frequently at a high level of arousal on the basis of their studies of autistic children's behaviour and concomitant E.E.G. recordings.

Cue selection

Some of the ways in which the child's selective attention develops were described in Chapter 3. It was noted how initially the child's attention was determined by certain salient stimulus features, but that, when habituation began to occur, the child's attention came under the influence of stimulus discrepancy. Habituation was put forward as a process which indicated the establishment of schemata, on the basis of which a child might build up his concepts of a stable environment.

Disorders in selective attention are among the most frequently noted behavioural disabilities which children show. In this connection, it is therefore of interest to consider findings on individual differences in habituation rate among infants. McCall and Kagan (1970) presented fifteen-week old infants with triangular arrangements of three small toys. After a habituation series, one, two or three of the toys were replaced by other ones, and the infants' responses to these changes in the stimulus display were noted. McCall and Kagan found varieties of response among the infants, which were related to the rate at which the infants had habituated to the original display of toys. Those with faster habituation rates showed more discriminating response when the discrepant stimulus displays were presented. In the context of the account in Chapter 3, this finding could be taken to indicate individual differences in the establishment of schemata among the infants.

Lewis *et al.* (1969) presented infants aged between three and eighteen months with a display consisting of a single blinking light. These workers found a consistent increase in habituation rate within this age range. This finding suggests a relationship between maturation and habituation rate.

In another study, a relationship between complexity of stimulus and rate of habituation was found.

Lewis and his coworkers also report studies which indicated possible relationships between habituation rate and etiological variables. Lewis and Goldberg (1969) studied the amount of interaction between infants and their mothers, and found that the infants with faster habituation rates tended to have mothers who were more responsive to them. Such a finding does not, of course, necessarily imply a causal connection. In another study (Lewis et al. 1969), the authors found a relationship between infants' habitu-ation rate and their physical condition at birth, as assessed on the Apgar scale. This scale is intended to indicate the intactness of the infant at birth (Apgar and James 1962), and the findings indicated that infants with per-fect scores showed a faster habituation rate than those with less than perfect scores. Both of these studies thus indicate that faster habituation rate may be associated with more favourable histories.

Lewis (1970) reports follow-up studies in which faster habituation to a visual stimulus was found to be associated with more rapid learning of a discrimination task at forty-four months and with Stanford–Binet IQ at the same age.

These findings are consistent in their indication that faster habituation rates are associated with better cognitive development and greater intact-ness and maturation of the nervous system in infants. However, as yet they must clearly be taken as offering only preliminary indications, in view of the very complex factors involved in infant development. Kagan (1969) reports follow-up findings on seventy infant boys, in which the association between fast habituation rate and optimal cognitive development is not so un-equivocal. He states that 'infants who show rapid habituation of fixation time to visual stimuli at four months and rapid shifting of foci of attention with toys at eight months, are likely at twenty-seven months to have short epochs of involvement with objects and fast decision-times in situations having response uncertainty'.

While the significance of these findings about individual differences in habituation rate is still rather unclear, it is tempting to speculate about their application to disabilities in sensory organization in children. This can be illustrated in a study by Hutt and Hutt (1964). These workers compared the behaviour of hyperactive and non-hyperactive children. Their experi-ment involved only a small number of children, but it is of interest on account of the extensive data they report. The study contained three groups of children. Two groups were made up of children with manifest signs of C.N.S. defect (eight children in each group), and the third group contained twelve children without evidence of brain injury. One of the C.N.S. defect groups contained children clinically described as hyperactive and the other did not. The ages of the children in each group ranged from three to eight years. The children's spontaneous behaviour was observed under four conditions. The children were left, one at a time, in a well-lit room, empty except for immovable fixtures such as light switches and a sink. This constituted condition A. Condition B was the same, except that some play bricks were placed on the floor. In condition C, a 'friendly observer' sat in the room, but remained passive. In condition D, the observer encouraged the child to play with the bricks. The children were exposed to these conditions in random order for three minutes each, and various aspects of their behaviour were recorded. Figure 6.1 shows the mean attention span of the

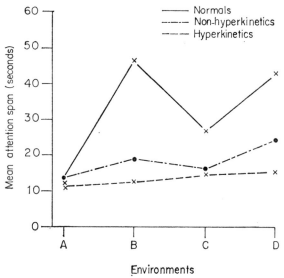

Figure 6.1. Mean attention span in four environmental settings. (Reproduced from Hutt, S. J. and Hutt, C. (1964), Hyperactivity in a group of epileptic (and some non-epileptic) brain-damaged children, *Epilepsia*, **5**, pp. 334–51, Fig. 3)

children in each group under the four conditions. Attention span was defined as the mean duration for which the child attended to a particular part of his environment in the room, whether it was the light switch, the 'friendly observer' or whatever. Except in condition A, the hyperactive group's attention span was always less, and it varied very little from one condition to another. The non-hyperactive groups' attention span, by contrast, varied directly with the scope for directed activity offered by the experimental setting. This is shown very clearly in Figure 6.2, in which the children's attention to specific items of the experimental settings is recorded. In conditions B, C and D, the non-hyperactive children attended almost exclusively to the blocks and to the friendly observer, while the hyperactive children still paid attention to the room fixtures.

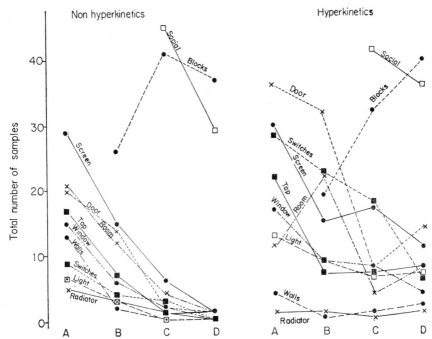

Figure 6.2. Frequency of attention to objects and people in four environmental settings. (Reproduced from Hutt, S. J. and Hutt, C. (1964), Hyperactivity in a group of epileptic (and some non-epileptic) brain-damaged children, *Epilepsia*, **5**, pp. 334–51, Fig. 7)

This descriptive analysis of the hyperactive and non-hyperactive children's behaviour lends itself to an explanation in terms of the individual differences in habituation rate and of 'richness' of schemata discussed above. The persistence of the hyperactive children's attention to the room fixtures could be related to the slow habituation of the children's orienting responses to the stimulus characteristics of their strange environment. Their brief play with the blocks and the observer correspondingly could be attributed to their poorly developed schemata. The converse of these explanations could be applied to the behaviour of the non-hyperactive children. The short attention span of these children under condition A corresponds to Kagan's suggestions mentioned in Chapter 3, since the familiarity of the fixtures provided no scope for 'perceptual assimilation'. Hutt and Hutt provide explanations of their subjects' behaviour in terms of a different theoretical model, which, in many ways, seems complementary to that offered here.

It is perhaps necessary to pause at this point to re-emphasize that the explanations offered for the children's behaviour are not the only possible ones, and that even those presented contain some conflicting aspects. For example, it might have been supposed that the superior schemata of the non-hyperactive children would have enabled them to find more of interest in a light switch or radiator. However, if these caveats are borne in mind, it may be profitable to pursue further the application of these theoretical formulations to the descriptions of children with deviant behaviour.

The descriptions of the behaviour of 'brain-injured' children provided by Cruickshank *et al.* (1961) and Strauss and his associates (1947, 1955) is similar to the behaviour of the children in the Hutts' experiment described above. Their proposals for remediation call for a reduction in stimulation of these children. It was argued that since the children are so distractible, they should be exposed only to stimuli relevant to what they are being taught. Cruickshank *et al.* (1961) attempted to evaluate an experimental teaching method planned along these lines. A 'distraction-free' classroom was set up in an ordinary school. The windows were glazed with frosted glass, and the floors and ceilings were covered in sound-proofing materials. All class apparatus was stored in closed cupboards, and all surfaces in the room were uniformly coloured. Booths were provided, in which children could work on their own, screened on three sides from extraneous stimulation. The teaching materials, by contrast, were designed to afford maximal stimulation. They were brightly coloured, with strongly emphasized configurations.

The teaching methods and classroom organization were very structured. The children were initially allowed little freedom in choice of activity, either during instruction or at other times. A carefully graded series of activities was planned for each child, according to his educational and behavioural level.

The experiment was carried out on children between the ages of seven and eleven, who were selected from ordinary schools on the basis of their behavioural manifestation of the 'Strauss syndrome' (distractibility, hyperactivity, etc.). The children were divided into an experimental and a control group. The experimental group were taught in the manner described above. The control group were taught in a special class in another ordinary school, but the choice of method was left to the teacher's discretion.

It should be emphasized that this is a simplified description of a study which in fact was very complex in its design and execution. For the purposes of this discussion, it is sufficient, however, to point out that control of intensity of stimulation and structured planning of activity were the salient features of the educational approach. When the control and experimental groups' progress were compared at the end of the school year, few statistically significant differences were found. The experimental group showed significantly accelerated progress only in figure-ground discrimination and on a measure of social maturity, but there was a tendency for the group to score higher on most measures.

The results of this extensive educational intervention did not, therefore provide support for the reduction of sensory stimulation. While an increasing number of educators are coming to stress the importance of structure in the education of distractible children (see, for example, Hewett 1968), there is little support for the emphasis on exclusion of sensory stimulation. Reduction of *level* of stimulation does not seem so important as avoidance of *change* in level of stimulation, if one is planning a distraction-reduced environment. A change from intense to slight stimulation is as attention evoking as an increase in stimulation. If one hypothesizes that habituation of the orienting response in the distractible child is slow, then avoidance of change in irrelevant features of his environment is likely to be of most help to him in the control of his attention. Therefore, it may well have been the case that the classroom environment of Cruickshank's control group was little more distracting to the children than that of the experimental group. A study by Brown (1966) provides some support for such a view. He carried out an experiment on subnormal children aged between four and eleven years attending a day Training Centre. He compared the rate at which they learnt to complete a form board when they were taught in their normal classroom, with the rate at which they learnt the task when taken out of their class to a quiet room on their own. In both settings the children were given individual instruction. Brown found that, on average, the learning rate of the children taught in a quiet room was slightly below that of the children taught in the classroom. Brown suggests that, although the noise and activity in the classroom was considerable, the children had habituated to it, and consequently were less distracted by it than by the different, though less intense, level of stimulation of the quiet room.

In this connection, it is also relevant to mention the strong aversion which some autistic children show to changes in environments with which they are familiar. Parents of autistic children sometimes describe how their children become very upset if the furniture in their home is moved around. Such behaviour may indicate an almost conscious attempt to 'ward off' a disruption of a background setting to which they have habituated. Hutt and Hutt (1970) describe the behaviour of autistic children who were introduced into a room with which they were familiar, but which contained a metal box (a piece of manipulation apparatus) which they had not seen before. The autistic children initially ignored the box studiously, even to the extent of sitting down with their backs to it. They also engaged in stereotypies (such as hand-flicking). The mean interval between entering the room and approaching the box was 441 seconds for the autistic children, compared with 108 seconds for the control group of children.

The studies described above indicate how individual differences in cue selection might be seen as the direct or indirect consequences of variations in the rate of habituation of orienting responses, and as contributing to the complexity of the perceptual schemata the child has built up. The studies have indicated that abnormally slow habituation of the orienting response may interfere with the establishment of schemata.

These findings can contribute to our understanding of the behavioural problems of distractible children. However, no mention has yet been made of the ways in which children may attempt to compensate for their difficulties and of the ways in which they can be helped to compensate. Intersensory integration and the use of language are two important sources of potential compensation. Intersensory integration is discussed in the following section, and the contribution of language will be discussed later.

Intersensory integration

The development of intersensory integration was discussed in the chapter on normal development, and the increasing role of the distance receptors of hearing and vision was outlined.

The association between vision and touch is an important one in the child's exploration of his environment. At an early stage the child learns to use vision to control his reaching movements (Piaget 1952, White 1967). Similarly, pointing becomes a means of directing visual attention. Fellows (1968), for example, describes how children were better able to discriminate between two patterns when they were allowed to point to them. Tactile exploration of an object can also extend visual attention in a number of ways. As a child moves his fingers about an object, his tactile exploration through its 'directing' function, can maintain his visual attention. If the child is exploring an object which can be manipulated, his manipulation will move the object about. This will produce changing visual stimulation, and these changes will, in turn, maintain the child's visual attention on it. In these various ways visual-tactile exploration can enable the distractible child to maintain the stimulus value of the object to which he is attending, relative to the stimulus value of irrelevant features of his environment. Given adequate intersensory integration the child's sensory organization might improve, but possibly at a slower rate.

Intersensory integration may itself be impaired. Goldfarb (1964) cites findings indicating poor intersensory integration among autistic children. He and his coworkers found that these children were no better at locating parts of their body which had been touched when they were permitted to do this visually, than when they were blindfolded. Impairment of intersensory integration between vision and other modalities seems likely to delay the establishment of vision as the main modality the child uses in his exploration of his environment. This might be a contributory factor in persistence of tactile exploration among the hyperactive children in the Hutts' study cited above.

Training in intersensory integration is included in some remedial programmes (for example, Tansley 1967) but, as far as I am aware, no evaluation studies have been carried out to assess its effects on improving behavioural adequacy.

Analysis

It has already been emphasized that sensory organization is an ongoing process. Successive 'cue selections' are, so to speak, 'worked on' until the sensory input either ceases or has been assimilated. 'Analysis' presumably occurs at each successive cue selection. As mentioned in Chapter 3, relatively little is known about this process and, because of the ongoing nature of sensory organization, it is difficult to distinguish cue selection and analysis. One disability which can be associated with this function is impaired figure-ground discrimination. This has mainly been studied experimentally (Strauss and Lehtinen 1947; Cruickshank *et al.* 1965) and so 'disability' has usually been defined in terms of the lower performance of a 'brain-injured' group of children. The experimental situations typically require the subject to identify a two-dimensional figure set against a figured background (Maslow *et al.* 1964; Cruickshank *et al.* 1965). The figures may be exposed briefly in a tachistoscope or presented without a time limit. Disturbance of figure-ground discrimination is then inferred if the child is unable to name the relevant figure correctly (in the Syracuse test) or to trace it (in the Frostig test). Some studies also compare the child's ability to name the figure when it is presented with and without a background (Strauss and Lehtinen 1947). The disability is sometimes described as a preferential response to 'ground', but it seems much more likely that Cruickshank is right in judging it to be a disability in discrimination. The task seems to depend on the extent to which the child can be flexible in his reorganization of the sensory input with successive cue selections. A deficit in such flexibility in visual analysis has been demonstrated in brain-injured children's recognition of reversible figures (Spivack and Levine 1957). In this experiment a child was shown figures such as those in Figure 6.3 (a) and (b), and asked to report whether he saw changes in the orientation of the cube, or alternations between faces in the left and right side of the circle.

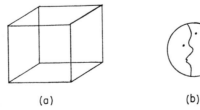

(a)   (b)

Figure 6.3. Patterns used for studying fluctuations in figure-ground discrimination

Difficulty in figure-ground discrimination appears to be limited to two-dimensional displays. Presumably movement parallax (the contrasting movement of foreground and background when the observer moves) provides a sufficient clue for discrimination in three-dimensional displays. Zuk (1962) in fact suggested that part of a brain-injured child's hyperactivity might be attributable to the child's attempts to induce movement parallax to help his organization of his visual sensory input. This suggestion possibly overstates the case, but it would be analogous to one of the suggested purposes of tactile exploration proposed above.

Difficulty in figure-ground discrimination has been given as an explanation of the difficulty some children experience in making sense of illustrations in books, and in using the guidelines of crayoning books. Frostig's perceptual programme (Frostig and Horne 1964) includes remedial methods for difficulties in figure-ground discrimination. She recommends exercises in which the child, for example, traces along one line that crosses over another. Presumably here the finger movement involved in tracing the line with a pencil acts as an aid in selective visual attention, and the continuity of the movement avoids confusion with the intersecting line. These exercises have been found to improve children's performance on the tests (Rosen 1966) but I am not aware of studies investigating the effect of this training on children's performance on other than specifically educational tasks.

Werner and Strauss (1941) claimed to demonstrate impairment in tactile figure-ground discrimination. They required children to explore by touch a grid arrangement of metal- and rubber-headed tacks—the rubber-headed tacks being positioned so as to represent a geometric shape. The children were then asked to draw the shapes represented by the rubber tacks. 'Brain-injured' children were found to include the metal tacks more frequently in their drawings, and to reproduce the geometric shape less frequently than a group of control children. The findings are, however, not conclusive, since possible differences in the children's pattern copying were not controlled.

A related disability termed 'astereognosis' has been found in cerebral palsied (Woods 1957) and certain other groups of children. In this task, common objects such as keys, pencils, rubbers, etc., are placed in a child's hand out of his sight and he is required to name the objects by feeling them. Although disability in this task is sometimes associated with loss in tactile sensitivity, it is also found where sensory loss is not regarded as sufficient to account for poor performance. The analysis in this and in Werner and Strauss's (1941) experiment involves the integration of successive tactile stimuli as the child moves his fingers about the object. Piaget and Inhelder (1956) and Zinchenko and Lomov (1960) have shown how this ability is gradually acquired by children, and how it appears to depend on the degree to which tactile exploration is carried out in a systematic way. Difficulty in this task may be another example of the inadequate establishment of schemata, on the basis of which the child can organize the movements in his tactile exploration.

General comments on disabilites of sensory organization

So far, this chapter has reviewed the evidence for the existence of different types of perceptual disability and has traced their potential effect on behavioural adequacy. It is necessary now to set these findings in the wider context of the child's development.

It will be evident that the various disabilities described can seriously limit a child in building up his concept of a stable and meaningful environment. On the other hand, these consequences are likely to be greatly modified by skilled maternal handling, particularly in the first few years. The mother can help the child to organize his environment by structuring his experience (M. Lewis 1970). For example, M. L. Barrett and M. H. Jones (1967) describe a multisensory training procedure used with cerebral-palsied nursery children between $1\frac{1}{2}$ and 5 years. In this procedure, the therapist tells a story about a child's activities and presents the child with the objects mentioned in the story, such as a hair brush, a ball, a wet rag, etc. In each case the child is encouraged to explore the object, while the therapist simultaneously utters the relevant descriptive adjectives such as smooth, round, soft, wet, etc. This kind of guided experience clearly helps the child to organize his sensory input and many mothers, if they have the time, include this type of activity in their play with their children. Talking to the child is, of course, one of the most important constituents of this activity. The naming of both the objects and their qualities provides a framework for the child to organize his experience (Vygotsky 1963) and, as Luria (1961) has shown, helps him to discriminate and identify. Emphasis on speech also helps the child to learn to attend to speech sounds and the one-to-one relationship between adult and child optimizes the child's attention.

Help within the home, or from outside, may thus mitigate the effects of disabilities on sensory organization. At the same time, one must remember that, to varying degrees, sensory and motor organization develops in all children whatever the degree of their difficulty (Wedell 1961, Birch 1964). Such development tends to be delayed, and this means that the child is out of step with the expectations of performance which his peers, family and school may have at any given developmental stage. This can lead to considerable misunderstanding and frustration. Frostig (1963) found that a high proportion of children showing poor adjustment in kindergarten made low scores on her perceptuo-motor tests. By second grade, this was the case with only half of the children and she suggests that children were becoming more successful in compensating for their difficulties.

Similar indications emerge from a study by Rubin and Braun (1968). These workers used a checklist to assess maladjustment in 4,500 children aged between six and eleven years in ordinary schools in a town in Michigan, USA. They identified 200 children with IQs over 80 showing the most numerous or most severe symptoms, and gave these children a battery of tests, including perceptuo-motor tests (for example, Bender Gestalt Test, Frostig Development Test of Perception). Rubin and Braun found that the distribution of the maladjusted group's combined scores on the cognitive and perceptuo-motor tests was bimodal. In other words, the group contained a substantial proportion of children with cognitive and perceptuo-motor disabilities, and this trend was more marked among the younger children.

Motor organization disability and behavioural adequacy

A major difference between sensory and motor organization disabilities lies in the opportunities for compensation open to the child. In the previous section it was emphasized that the child uses the whole range of sensory information open to him in building up his concepts about his environment, supplementing, for example, by tactile perception what he cannot achieve by visual perception. This means that the degree of a disability in any one sensory modality does not entail a corresponding disturbance of the whole system of sensory organization. Motor organization, on the other hand, constitutes the 'final common path' to voluntary action. Although such activity is manifested in many different ways—for example in speech, gesture and locomotion—it is still dependent on the processes of motor organization. Any degree of deficiency in motor organization is consequently more immediately apparent to other people and more handicapping to the child.

Brenner and Gillman (1966) made a study of the perceptuo-motor skills of eight-year-old Cambridge schoolchildren. They mainly used tests involving motor as well as sensory organization, and found that many of the children who showed specific disability were described by their teachers as untidy and clumsy in gross and fine movement. Brenner et al. (1967) made a closer study of fourteen of the children showing specific disability. Only one of these children expressed any interest in hobbies requiring fine motor control (such as carpentry or sewing), compared with eleven out of fourteen control children. Gubbay et al. (1965) also described a group of fourteen children who showed difficulty in dressing and pattern copying among other problems. Children with these disabilities are often dubbed as stupid by other children and by adults since they show no physical handicap which might account for their inadequacy, but none of the studies cited found a correlation between sensory and motor organization and tested 'intelligence'. The extent to which these children are misjudged probably contributes to the degree of emotional disturbance which Rubin and Braun (1968) found among them in their study.

Children with motor organization disabilities are most commonly identified after they start school, when their inadequacy is highlighted by the
more specific level of performance expected of them. However, parents'
retrospective reports usually show that the problem existed earlier.

Three main aspects of motor organization will be dealt with here:
hyperactivity, lateralization in motor organization, and pattern copying.

Hyperactivity

Many writers (for example, Eisenberg 1966) have described 'hyperactive'
children, and they have already been mentioned in the previous section.
These are children who show extreme restlessness and have difficulty in
settling down to activities in which they are expected to be still. The Hutts'
experiment, already cited, showed how children judged clinically as hyperactive failed to modify their behaviour when given opportunities for focused
activity. They found that their 'hyperactive' children moved around the
experimental room more under every condition except the first one (condition A). In their experiment movement was assessed by the number of
times a child crossed the lines of a grid marked on the floor of the experimental room. Schulman *et al.* (1965) assessed the activity rate of mentally
retarded children over a period of several days, measuring the children's
activity with modified self-winding wrist watches. They found that children
differed in their activity rates, but that, whether high or low, these activity
rates were fairly consistently maintained. They did not find a difference
between the activity rates of children with and without evidence of brain
damage. Schulman *et al.* postulated that children's activity rate was not
so much a reaction to specific situations as an independent behavioural
trait characterizing the child. This view appears to conflict with Hutt and
Hutt's findings, which suggested that the differences between the behaviour
of hyperactive and non-hyperactive children varied with the situation in
which the children were placed. However, Schulman *et al.* did not include
a control group in their study, and so were not able to note the similarity
of activity of hyperactive and non-hyperactive children in an unstimulating
setting such as condition A in the Hutts' experiment.

It seems likely that hyperactivity does not occur only as a concomitant
of short attention span. Most teachers and clinicians are familiar with
children who appear to have a greater than usual need for activity. These
children can often be helped by being allowed to move around energetically
at intervals. They then appear to be able to remain still for a while.
Explanations other than the circular one that these children have greater
'activity drive' do not yet appear to be available. It is evident, however,
that hyperactivity is more frequently found among boys than among girls
(Leydorf 1971).

Hyperactivity has been discussed here, since it is such a clear example of disorganized motor activity. However, the explanations offered above suggest that it should be considered a consequence of other disabilities, rather than a disability of motor organization itself.

Lateralization in motor organization

One of the most commonly found types of motor organization disability is confusion in using and identifying limbs on either side of the body. In a group of children identified as being excessively clumsy, as measured on the Oseretsky scale, Yule (1967) found 64·5 per cent to have difficulty in right–left discrimination, compared with 32 per cent of his control subjects. The children were aged between nine and eleven. Left–right discrimination was measured by asking the child to carry out lateralized movements (for example, 'Point to your nose with your left hand') and by asking him to point to the examiner's body (for example, 'Point to my right hand'). Performance of this task is, of course, also dependent on language comprehension, but it seems likely that in Yule's study the children were too old for this to be a limiting factor. Brenner *et al.* (1967) found that their eight-year-old children with specific perceptuo-motor disability were poorer than their controls on the same type of left-right discrimination, but the difference was not statistically significant. Gubbay *et al.*'s (1965) disability group were also poor on left–right discrimination, but the authors do not mention how this was assessed.

Ayres (1965) found that the performance on a posture copying task of a group of six- to eight-year-old schoolchildren with learning difficulties was poorer than that of a control group. Her task did not involve verbal instructions, and so excluded any possible effects of language difficulties. However, performance was scored for speed as well as accuracy.

A study which attempted to isolate some of the effective components in treatment of poor left–right discrimination was carried out by Hill *et al.* (1967). They gave mentally retarded children training in left–right discrimination, and compared its effectiveness when given with verbal formulation and when given without. Equal improvement was found under both conditions, and the authors concluded that the disability was not secondary to language defects.

Disability in copying lateralized movements has been ascribed to defects in 'body image'. Defective 'body image' has, in turn, been ascribed to unestablished lateral hand, eye and foot preference (Delacato 1963), but Benton (1959) found little evidence for this. Furthermore, Robbins (1966) found that the lateral preference of second-grade children was less developed after four months of the treatment advocated by Delacato than it had been before.

Both lateral preference and left–right discrimination are, of course, found to increase with age in the course of normal development. It seems conceivable that disabilities in both may be independent consequences of developmental delay in other functions.

Disorganization of movements involving limbs on either side of the body does appear to persist in an isolated form, even in children who are only moderately awkward. Kephart (1960) described children who have difficulty in alternate hopping, and J. F. Keogh (1968) described children who have difficulties in tapping alternately with one finger of each hand.

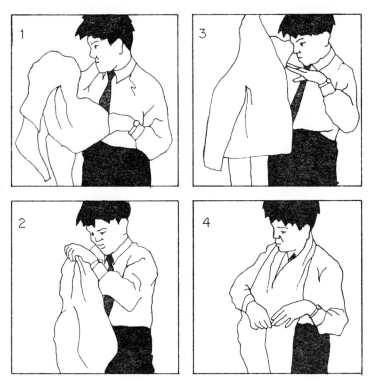

Figure 6.4. Successive stages in a twelve-year-old boy's attempts to put on a cardigan

Does difficulty in the left–right discrimination of movements constitute a handicap? Clearly this is related to the age to which it persists. Confusion in dressing is commonly found to be associated with this difficulty. It is reported by Gubbay et al. (1965) and is also frequently reported anecdotally. The film sequence in Figure 6.4 shows a twelve-year-old boy trying, but failing, to put on a cardigan by himself. His effector efficiency was adequate but he was unable to organize his movements appropriately. He was also unable to tie his shoe-laces. In this example the child is showing difficulty in working out the relationship between the spatial orientation of his own body and that of the cardigan. This illustrates the way in which one could speak of this difficulty as resulting from a failure in the establishment of 'body image' or 'schema'. This child's confusion suggests that he does not use his own body as a consistent point of reference in organizing his movements in space. In this context, 'body image' represents a constant element which emerges—perhaps in a cumulative way—from the sensory-motor feedback of the child's movements in space.

Disorganization of movement may also show itself in a wider spatial context. Holt and Reynell (1967) describe a boy who had difficulty in finding his way around a room, and case histories of children who get 'lost' in their school or their home area are familiar. Difficulty in finding one's way around is, of course, frequently reported in adults, who report using verbal self-instruction to maintain the necessary sequence of directional movements. Maps frequently fail to help these people, since they introduce the additional spatial problem of analysing the map itself. B. K. Keogh and J. F. Keogh (1967) investigated a related aspect of children's performance. They asked ESN boys (IQ 51–77, mean CA 10,3) to 'walk' a pattern presented to them as a diagram on a card. The mean score of the ESN group was slightly lower than that of the six-year-old children in the control group described in Chapter 3. Twenty-six per cent of the ESN group children scored less than the average six-year-old control child. The authors report that the ESN group's poor performance was not due to failure to understand the task, since all of the children managed to walk the trial circle presented before testing. All the subjects were also asked to copy the patterns, and their copies were scored for accuracy in a similar way to the 'walked' patterns. The ESN children's performance on copying the patterns was also poorer, but they found the walking task particularly hard. The Keogh's walking task involves a multiplicity of skills, but their description of how the ESN children set about it indicates that difficulty in spatial orientation presented a major problem. The ESN boys 'seemed to have difficulty in planning their movements or organizing their actions. They walked without any clearly defined reference points, seemed unsure when a directional change should be made or when they should stop. Some became confused and walked about the room almost at random.'

An interesting feature of this orientation task is that the child has to relate each successive movement to all his previous movements, since the spatial relationships between himself and his environment alter with his successive positions.

A third aspect of motor organization involves the timing and temporal sequence of movement. Timing is involved particularly in ball games, where the child has to match his actions to the rate of movement of the ball. Kephart mentions this as a specific aspect of motor organization disability. The film sequence in Figure 6.5 shows a ten-year-old boy

Figure 6.5. Successive stages in a ten-year-old boy's attempts to catch a ball

attempting to catch a ball being thrown to him on two occasions. It is clear that he is making the correct movements, but at the wrong time. This kind of disability is certainly likely to be a handicap to a child, since ball games play such an important part in our culture. Survival in city traffic is, of course, also dependent on accurate timing of movement.

Movement in temporal sequence has been studied by J. F. Keogh (1968). He investigated the hopping performance of seven-year-old children. The children were required to hop twice on each alternate foot five times in succession. Keogh also assessed the children's performance on some of the component tasks, such as recognizing patterns of tapped rhythms and balancing and hopping on the same foot. Children who failed the main hopping task differed in their relative performances on the component tasks. Some of the children did not appear to be aware of the number of times their legs had moved, even though they were quite able to count. Other children had difficulty in switching from one to the other foot in the hopping sequence, and had to stand on both feet for the interchange. This suggests that incorporating movements of limbs on both sides in a sequence presents an additional problem as mentioned above.

Disabilities in a variety of motor tasks have been described. Many of the tasks are trivial in themselves, but they are representative of skills which are important to the child's development. Parents judge their children by their self-help skills, such as dressing. Children's standing among their peers depends very much on their skill at games and other activities requiring motor organization. The child himself can obtain great satisfaction from skilled physical activity. Symes (1971) carried out an investigation of the social acceptance of clumsy boys aged eleven to thirteen in an English grammar school. The clumsy boys were those who scored lowest in their year group on various motor skills related to games performance. In each class boys were asked to list those whom they were least likely to choose for a sports team, and those they would choose to accompany them on holiday. The choices for the clumsy children were compared with those for other children randomly chosen in the same class. The results as might be expected showed that the clumsy boys were much less frequently (and in fact very rarely) chosen as co-members of sports teams. There was much less difference between the groups when chosen as holiday companions, although the clumsy children were still chosen less frequently. There is little doubt that disability in motor organization may seriously affect a child's image of himself, and make him regard himself as a failure. Such attitudes arising out of failure in motor skills are likely to lead to expectation of failure in other activities.

An aspect of motor organization which has been studied more than any other is pattern copying, and this will now be considered.

Pattern copying

The literature on pattern-copying disability in children is extensive, but the vast bulk of the work is concerned either with using performance on pattern-copying tasks as a diagnostic indication of 'brain injury' or as a predictor of reading readiness or as a concomitant of reading failure. The latter two areas of research will be considered in the next chapter, the first area is not directly relevant to this book. Little research has been done on pattern-copying disability in its own right.

In the pre-school child, poor pattern copying represents perhaps a limited potential handicap. Its real importance becomes evident as the performance demands of school approach. However, just as with the organization of bodily movement, many of the pre-school activities on which children's and adults' judgments of a child are based involve pattern copying. These activities include modelling, drawing, singing and constructional tasks; tasks which pre-school children of course also enjoy. Furthermore, it seems likely that practice in these types of activity is important for the further development of the skills and functions on which later academic attainment is based.

Many researchers, as has already been mentioned, used pattern-*copying* tasks to investigate *sensory organization* skills, and the ambiguity of such an inference has already been pointed out. The tasks used have ranged from pencil-and-paper copying to block construction; from the one-to-one correspondence of copying a block model, to the conventional representation inherent in pencil-and-paper copying.

Some research has been directed at identifying the causes of poor pattern copying. Cruickshank *et al*. (1965) included a marble board pattern-copying task in their study of the perceptuo-motor abilities of cerebral palsied and non-handicapped children. The children were presented with four boards with marbles arranged in patterns. On two of the boards the holes formed a regular grid (task A) and, on the other two boards, the holes were themselves arranged in a pattern (task B) thus providing potential distraction. The children were required to reproduce the marble patterns on empty boards. This study is of interest, since the researchers were concerned with evaluating not only the accuracy of the children's performance, but also their approach to the task when they completed it successfully. In task A, the spastic children tended to use an 'incoherent' rather than a 'methodical' approach more frequently than the other children. The patterns to be copied consisted of overlapping figures, and an 'incoherent' approach was one in which children did not systematically build up either the individual figure, or the outline of the combined figures. On task B, more children in all groups tended to use an 'incoherent' approach, and no significant difference was found between the groups. Some children who had used a methodical approach on task A, now performed in an incoherent way on task B. Although the design of Cruickshank *et al*.'s experiment does not provide conclusive evidence, the study does illustrate how the problem for the spastic children showing relative disability in task A was similar to that of the control children when faced with a more complex task. This suggests that the spastic children's difficulty lay mainly in the sensory organization of the pattern they were meant to be copying.

The critical disability in the above study contrasts interestingly with that found in a study by Bortner and Birch (1962). They investigated the performance of twenty-eight (CA 8–18) cerebral palsied children on the Wechsler Intelligence Scale for Children Block Design subtest. (In this test the child has to copy a two-dimensional coloured pattern with multi-coloured blocks.) When a child had failed three consecutive designs testing was stopped. For any design on which the child failed, he was presented with a set of three designs made up of blocks—one design was the correct one, one the incorrect copy the child had made, and the third, another incorrect design. The child was then asked which of these block designs corresponded to the one on the stimulus card. Of the eighty-nine designs on which errors were made, the children were able to identify the correct copy in seventy instances. In other words, in this task, failure was more frequently due to an inability to reproduce the patterns than to discriminate them correctly. Wedell and Horne (1969) tried to identify the relative roles of visual discrimination and motor organization in pattern copying. They also compared pattern-copying performance with pencil and paper and with plasticine strips. The design of the study was based on that used in Wedell (1964) described in Chapter 3. The Bender Gestalt Test was given as a group test (B. K. Keogh and C. E. Smith 1961) to 150 children aged $5\frac{1}{2}$ in their first year at infant school. Using the scoring method devised by Keogh and Smith, the twenty children with the highest and the twenty with the lowest score were selected for further investigation. The children in these

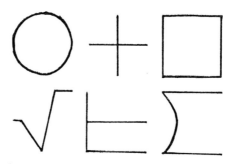

Figure 6.6. Six patterns used in a study of children's pattern copying

high (H) and low (L) scoring groups were given the tasks used in Wedell (1964), involving the same four designs and two additional ones (see Figure 6.6). The projection scoring method was used on all except the discrimination task. The graphs in Figure 6.7 show the distribution of scores on the tasks.

Only four of the children in the L group appeared to have difficulty in the visual discrimination of the patterns. These four, not surprisingly, also made poor scores on the pattern-copying tasks. If they could not discriminate the patterns, they could hardly be expected to copy them, as was illustrated in Cruickshank's study. All the children appeared to have eye-hand coordination sufficient to perform the copying tasks. Although the L group's tracing scores were poorer than the H group's, their lowest scores on the tracing task were still higher than any of the scores on the copying tasks (see Figure 6.7). The H and L group were differentiated more by their performance on the plasticine than by their performance on the pencil copying task, since the projection scoring method was more stringent than the Keogh and Smith method used on the Bender figures.

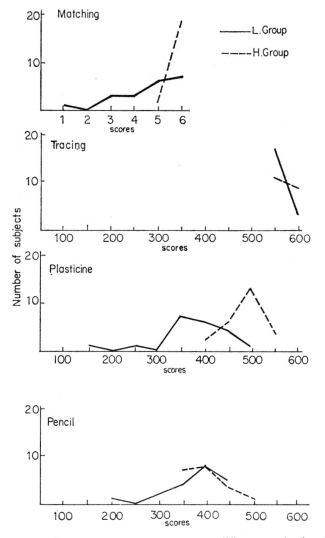

Figure 6.7. Distribution of accuracy scores on different tasks involving the same patterns

Pencil copying involves not only facility in using a pencil as a tool, but also familiarity with the conventions of drawing. The plasticine task, on the other hand, involves only one-to-one reproduction of a pattern, and Wedell and Horne regarded it as a more direct measure of motor organization, since the children were even provided with plasticine strips of the requisite length and number. Since the L group were little better on the plasticine than on the pencil copying task, it was argued that disability in motor organization was probably the main cause of their poor performance on the pencil copying task.

In this connection it is interesting to compare the L group's relative scores on these tasks, with those of the average 3¾-year-old children in the Wedell (1964) study. The 3¾-year-old children's mean error scores on both the eye-hand coordination and visual discrimination tasks were higher, and more level with their error scores on the copying tasks. The L group's pattern of performance thus does not correspond to that of younger children. For a majority of the L group, poor motor organization appears to be the major disability. In a minority of cases, performance seems to be limited by poor visual discrimination, although motor organization may, of course, be poor as well. Wedell and Horne stress that their conclusions must be regarded as tentative, since these are based on a very small sample of subjects, and depend on the validity of the scoring method used. The findings are, however, consistent with the findings of Bortner and Birch (1962), Maslow *et al.* (1964) and Ayres (1965), in showing that poor performance on pattern-copying tasks may be due to disability in particular component skills.

A further question about specificity of disability concerns the types of error made in the copying of patterns. Does sensory or motor organization difficulty affect some spatial characteristics rather than others? This question has been studied mainly in terms of differences between 'brain-injured' children and controls. Bensberg (1952) found that 'brain-injured' children's Bender Test copies contained more reversals and perseverations (repeated parts of patterns). These children also had difficulty in forming angles, and substituted lines for dots. Halpin and Patterson (1958) found that their group of 'brain-injured' children did not make more reversals than controls on a 'concrete' copying test (Goldstein–Scheerer Stick Test). Their 'brain-injured' group did, however, make more rotations, a characteristic error also found by Shapiro (1953) on the Koh's Block Design Test. Needless to say, all of these studies also report that a higher proportion of 'brain-injured' children make unrecognizable pattern copies.

Relatively few studies have investigated *visual discrimination* of non-literal shapes, and even fewer have analysed the types of error made. Wedell (1960a) in his study of cerebral palsied children, did not find that these made significantly more reversal or rotation errors on a visual discrimination task than his control group. Berko (1954) compared the performance of twenty cerebral palsied and twenty control children (mean CA 9,7, mean IQ 80) on the Seguin Form Board. The cerebral palsied children made many more errors (ninety compared with eight). Fifty-four of the errors made by the cerebral palsied children involved failure to discriminate angles. Thirty of these were confusions between the square and the diamond shape, twenty between the rectangle and elongated hexagon. Although these studies used very different tasks and materials, they do suggest that certain spatial characteristics do present particular difficulty. Rotation and reversal errors appear to occur more frequently in pattern copying than in visual discrimination tasks, and may be secondary to some of the spatial aspects of motor organization disability mentioned above.

So far the discussion has been only of pattern copying. Spontaneous drawing and pattern construction have most commonly been used for psycho-diagnostic purposes (see, for example, Lowenfeld 1929, Goodenough 1926, etc.). The Manikin (Merrill–Palmer Scale), Object Assembly (Wechsler Intelligence Scale for Children), Make-a-Face (Albitreccia 1958) and Draw-a-Person tests have been used in the study of spontaneous pattern construction. Wedell (1960a) used the Manikin and Face tests with the children in his study of cerebral palsied children. The children were presented with six wooden Manikin pieces and asked to 'put them together to make a boy'. For the face test, the children were presented with two sets of ingredients (eyes, nose, mouth and eyebrows) and told to arrange them on a blank felt face (see Figure 6.8). Both tasks were scored on fairly

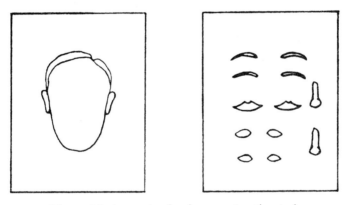

Figure 6.8. Apparatus for face construction task

lenient all-or-none criteria. The reasons for failure appear to be rather varied, as can be seen from Figures 6.9 and 6.10. Most of the children were given a second attempt at these tasks, if they failed to satisfy the criterion on the first attempt. The child in Figure 6.9 appears to have had little idea how to do the task spontaneously (1). When given a demonstration, he arranged the ingredients correctly (2). Two and three quarter years later, he was able to complete the task correctly at first attempt (3). The child in Figure 6.10 appeared to have no idea how to put the Manikin together (1), but made a reasonable attempt after demonstration (2). Two and a half years later, he produced a 'human-like' Manikin spontaneously (3). Adequate initial performance on these tasks presumably depends on

Figure 6.9. A child's attempts to construct a face (1) spontaneously, (2) after a demonstration, (3) two and a half years later. (From Wedell, K. (1961), Follow-up study of perceptual ability in children with hemiplegia, *Little Clubs Clinics in Developmental Medicine*, **4**, pp. 76–85, by permission of Spastics International Medical Publications)

adequate visual imagery to guide the child's actions. Considering that the children's first and second attempts were both dependent on motor organization, the differences in performance can be taken to indicate the effect of deficiency in imagery.

Children's spontaneous human figure drawings have been investigated by Goodenough (1926) and Harris (1963), among others. Many approaches to the evaluation of such drawings have been made, but none have been concerned with figure drawing as a measure purely of sensory and motor organization. Several workers have claimed to find that physically handicapped children draw human figures which portray their particular handicap. However, neither Silverstein and Robinson (1956) nor Abercrombie and Tyson (1966) were able to distinguish the figure drawings of physically

Figure 6.10. A child's attempts to construct a manikin figure (1) spontaneously, (2) after a demonstration, (3) two and a half years later. (From Wedell, K. (1961), Follow-up study of perceptual ability in children with hemiplegia, *Little Clubs Clinics in Developmental Medicine*, **4**, pp. 76–85, by permission of Spastics International Medical Publications)

handicapped children from those of non-handicapped children, when these were judged 'blind'. In general, it appears that poor human figure drawings are directly the consequence of deficiency in visual imagery and disability in motor organization.

Remedial programmes

One might expect that studies of the effectiveness of sensory and motor organization training programmes would provide a useful source of information about the relevance of sensory and motor organization skills to behavioural adequacy. Unfortunately, evaluatory studies, although increasing, are still relatively few. Adequate evaluation of a training programme requires long-term research, which is difficult to fit in with the requirements of the 'Ph.D. industry'.

However, the training programmes themselves often do not make evaluation easy. Training programmes may be divided into two main categories.

(a) Programmes aimed at the improvement of specific skills (for example the discrimination of reversed figures) as ends in themselves. These objectives consequently tend to be too specific to provide evidence of the relevance of sensory and motor organization disabilities to behavioural adequacy, and the studies do not usually include investigations of more general transfer effects.

(b) Programmes which, while aimed at more general behavioural or educational adequacy, are more particularly directed at skills which are presumed to underlie behavioural adequacy. These programmes imply that improvement on the specific skills will transfer to the 'target' behaviour. A very common 'target' behaviour is, of course, educational attainment and, in particular, reading ability. Evidence on this will be considered in the next chapter. Although behavioural adequacy is usually stated as one of the main objectives of these programmes, attempts to evaluate the attainment of these objectives are practically never made. Such evaluation would certainly present methodological difficulties, but there appears to have been little acknowledgement even of the need for such evaluation. Frequently, demonstration of improvement in the skills at which the programmes are specifically directed—for example, the performance of certain movements —seems to have been regarded as sufficient validation; the transfer to more general skills presumably being regarded as too obvious to need proof.

Programmes aimed at very specific skills

Fellows (1968) describes two studies which indicated the role of movement in the establishment of visual discrimination of pattern reversals. Newson (1955) was concerned to overcome five-year-old children's difficulty in discriminating the single reversed figure in a set of six—that is, in spotting the 'odd one out'. She gave the children a graded series of exercises. These, in sequence, consisted of: (1) pointing in the direction of movement illustrated in pictures, (2) fitting pieces into a form board in the correct direction, and (3) using wire figure outlines of reversible figures as a guide to discriminating orientation difference in the original task. Each child was given 20 minutes' training for 5 days. On retesting with the original test, she found that the children who had been given her training sequence performed significantly better than a control group of children, who had only practised the original discrimination task. However, Fellows points out that no information was given about the transfer of this skill to educational or general behavioural performance.

Jeffrey (1958) found that he was unable to teach 3,11–4,9-year-old children to distinguish successively two stick figures of men with one arm up and the other down. The children were required to call one figure 'Jack' and the figure with the reversed arm position, 'Jill'. Jeffrey then presented the figures on a board, with push buttons to left and right of the figure. He asked the children to push the button to which the figure's raised arm pointed. He found that the children quickly learnt to do this, and were subsequently able to learn the original naming task without the use of the push buttons. Interestingly, however, he experienced difficulty in preventing the children from continuing to push the buttons, and found that some children persisted in making small movements. Fellows suggests that the children may have mastered the task by responding, even if only covertly, to the figure and then naming the figure. The child's learned motor response was thus 'added' to the total discrimination situation and, with this added clue, the child was able to make the correct discrimination.

Fellows (1968) also reports a study by Bijou, in which children aged between three and seven, and a group of retarded children (CA 6,4–16,11, MA 3,10–8,10) were taught to discriminate pattern reversals purely by visual means. The children were given a very carefully graded series of multiple-choice visual discriminations. In the course of this, their discrimination response was 'shaped' from initial shape discrimination to final discrimination of reversals in different orientations. The majority of the children in both groups succeeded in learning the discrimination, and furthermore were able to transfer it to other patterns. Bijou's study suggests that, given sufficiently careful grading of the material, discrimination can be taught without using movement as a clue. However, it would be interesting to know whether there is any difference in the transfer of the discrimination taught by the two methods. Although all these three studies included limited transfer training, this was not tested to a wide range of generality. However, systematic training for transfer is clearly an essential part of these training procedures, and it is often noticeable by its absence in the more general studies to be discussed below. The three studies provide an interesting example of the way in which 'cue selection' can be systematically induced, and Jeffrey's study shows how a response to a discrimination task can itself be used as a cue.

Wedell (1965) reports a study in which children aged $3\frac{3}{4}$ and $5\frac{1}{4}$ years were given training in the visual discrimination of patterns, and the transfer of this training to the copying of the patterns was assessed. The patterns were the same as those shown in Figure 6.6, and the multiple-choice visual discrimination patterns the same as those used by Wedell (1964). The children were given a maximum of six visual-discrimination training sessions, during which they were required to match the patterns. They were told when they were right and corrected when they were wrong. Apart from this, no verbal help was given. The children's pencil-and-paper copies of the patterns, as well as their matching performance, were assessed before and after the training. In the $5\frac{1}{4}$-year age group, the experimental group made a significantly greater improvement in both matching and copying than the control group. There were no significant differences among the $3\frac{3}{4}$-year-old children. Figure 6.11 (a) and (b) shows some of the changes in the pattern copying of children in both age groups. It is interesting to note the beginnings of a differentiated response in the poorer pattern copies of the $3\frac{3}{4}$-year-old children. The study suggests that pattern copying in children may be improved if they are given some idea of the relevant stimulus dimensions.

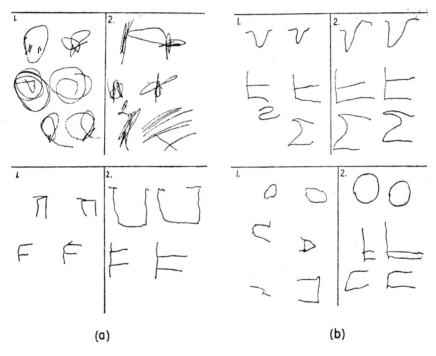

(a)   (b)

Figure 6.11. (a) Attempts to copy patterns (1) before and (2) after visual discrimination training by $3\frac{3}{4}$-year-old children in experimental group, (b) Attempts to copy patterns (1) before and (2) after visual discrimination training by $5\frac{1}{4}$-year-old children in experimental group. The patterns in (a) are 1, 3, 6, 4, 5 and in (b) are 4, 5, 6, 1, 5, 6, (see Figure 6.6). From Shape discrimination and shape copying, Loring (ed), *Teaching the Cerebral Palsied Child*, 1965, Heinemann

A project aimed at applying operant conditioning to movement defect is reported by Connolly (1968). He was concerned to improve the accuracy of reaching movements in a cerebral palsied child. Connolly produced an apparatus that consisted of a clown's face with a large hole for a mouth. The size of this hole could be made progressively smaller. It was planned that the child should learn to put his hand in the clown's mouth with increasing accuracy as the hole was made smaller. A successful reaching movement would be rewarded by the clown's eyes lighting up. Connolly saw the main skill that the child needed to acquire as the ability to reach accurately without visual 'monitoring' of the movement, through the increased use of kinesthetic feedback.

Programmes aimed at general behavioural and educational adequacy

The effectiveness of sensory and motor organization programmes directed particularly at furthering educational progress will be discussed in Chapter 7. However, it is not premature to mention that the transfer found to specific educational skills is in general found to be slight, and so the studies are possibly more profitably discussed in the present context of behavioural adequacy. A large number of treatment programmes have been devised (see Tansley 1967 and the summary by Myers and Hammill 1969). Discussion here will mainly be confined to those programmes on which evaluation studies have been carried out. These programmes deal with visual rather than auditory sensory organization disabilities. Although programmes for auditory discrimination exist (see, for example, Barry 1961), either they have not, to my knowledge, been experimentally evaluated or they are primarily directed at language training (Kirk 1966) and so come outside the frame of reference of this book.

Some programmes aim at the improvement of the child's general sensory and motor organization by activities which are intended to affect his neurophysiological efficiency. Delacato and his associates (see Delacato 1963) postulate that human neurological development follows the sequence of phylogenetic development. Their programme thus requires the child with sensory and motor organization disability to proceed through exercises in successive postural positions, corresponding to phylogenetic stages, so that his neurological development can be furthered. A central feature of the programme is the establishment of assymetrical motor skills (such as the alternating movements of arms and legs in crawling). Delacato's method involves intensive work with children and their parents, with the aim that treatment should be continuous. Delacato cites studies of the effectiveness of his method. His theoretical standpoint has, however, been criticized and systematic evaluation studies (Robbins 1966, Kerschner 1968) have not substantiated the claims made for his methods. Robbins, for example, in the study cited earlier found that after four months of training, a group of second-grade (seven- to eight-year-old) children showed less laterilization of motor skill than at the start. Kerschner's study of retarded children showed that an experimental group given five months of Delacato training were slightly better at creeping and crawling than a control group who were given a general physical education programme, but that there was no difference between the groups' performance on the Oseretsky Motor Development Test (a general test of motor skill). The effectiveness of the Delacato method thus seems open to question. One might argue, moreover, that such an intensive programme would, if it were effective, hardly be likely to lead to such conflicting findings. These studies unfortunately do not throw light on the interaction between sensory and motor organization and behavioural adequacy.

Ayres (1968) also proposes a motor training programme aimed at improving neuro-physiological function. Her approach is based on physiotherapy, and traces poor motor organization to inadequate inhibition of infantile motor reflexes. Her aim is to improve children's neuro-physiological function in order to make them more adequate in the behavioural and educational achievement required of them. Ayres studied the progress of groups of eight-year-old children in special classes of ordinary schools who were given her programme additionally and compared it with the progress of children who were not given the programme. She found no overall benefit for the children who were given her programme. She measured the progress of her experimental and control group children on the Illinois Test of Psycholinguistic Abilities (ITPA), the Frostig Developmental Test of Visual Perception, and on her own battery of tests (the Southern California Battery). Children given her treatment showed only slightly greater improvement than the control children in bilateral motor coordination, imitation of postures, crossing the mid-line, motor accuracy, form board performance and Visual Decoding (ITPA). However, apparently teachers reported that the treated children were more competent in their play, and were noticeably more confident. While these relative improvements noted by teachers were not objectively assessed, they indicate that teacher ratings would provide valuable data. More extensive evaluation studies of the Ayres technique are in progress.

Kephart (1960) is concerned directly with the improvement of sensory and motor organization skills, which he asserts underlie the development of the child's spatial concepts and so affect his behavioural and educational adequacy. There are four basic aspects of motor organization which he regards as of particular significance; posture and the maintenance of balance, locomotion (moving from one point to another), contact (manipulation) and receipt and propulsion (catching, and the child's relation to moving objects in general). He provides an extensive battery of activities to foster these. Evaluatory studies have not supported the postulated benefit for reading attainment, but Cratty (1970) cites studies by Brown and by Haring and Stables in which improvement in the specific motor skills trained was found. Once again, information on transfer to more general behaviour is not given.

Frostig's programme (Frostig and Horne 1964), while recognizing the basic relevance of movement in general, is directed primarily at visual and visuo-motor activities. (A more recently published programme—Frostig and Maslow 1970—is aimed also at more general movement). Frostig postulates five main processes of visuo-motor function; eye-motor coordination, figure-ground discrimination, form constancy, position in space, and spatial relations. Her Developmental Test of Visual Perception is designed to assess each of these areas, and her training programmes consist of paper-and-pencil exercises corresponding to these. In general, the programme has been found to improve performance on the Frostig test. Studies have been reported on pre-school to adolescent children, and have included physically handicapped and retarded children (Rosen 1966, Horn and Quarmby 1970, Tyson 1963, Allen, Dickman and Haupt 1966). However, once again, transfer, where studied, has been related mainly to educational achievement. Frostig stresses the need to train for transfer of the specific skills included in her programme and also includes language and other training at her school.

The possible effect of sensory and motor organization training on 'cognitive style' is illustrated in a study by Berger (1969). Berger compared the impact of Montessori and of 'traditional' kindergarten methods on Head Start (socially deprived) classes of Puerto Rican and Negro children aged approximately 3 to 4½. She found that after one year the Montessori group had made greater progress only in specifically perceptual tasks. (This greater improvement was found mainly in the younger children and those whose performance on perceptual tasks had been low.) However, the Montessori group scored more highly on the Cincinnati Autonomy Test Battery, which is designed to measure such variables as "impulse control', 'task persistence', 'analytic style' and 'field independence'. The children were followed up after a further year, but these measures of cognitive style were unfortunately not included in the retest. The Montessori children were, however, found to pay more attention to fine visual detail and scored more highly on the Frostig 'Eye-motor 'and 'Figure-ground' subtests.

It is unfortunate that few programmes have explicitly been stated to be aimed at behavioural adequacy, since this seems a much more likely area of accrued benefit, and also of need. Edgar et al. (1969) report a small study of subnormal children, which suggests that sensory and motor organization training can be shown to affect behavioural adequacy. The children, aged three to eight (MA 1 to 2), were given training along the lines of Kephart's programme, and were tested on the Gesell scales before and after intervention. Compared to a control group (given nonspecific attention) the trained group made significantly more progress on all three of the Gesell subscales (motor, language and personal-social behaviour).

It is of prime importance to investigate the contributions, not only of the programmes as a whole, but also of their components. Most of the programmes are expensive in time, personnel and materials, so that components which do not contribute to remedial objectives cannot be justified. An example of a study which attempted to compare the effectiveness of different emphases in sensory and motor organization training is provided by Sisson (1967). She found that a programme emphasizing visual and auditory discrimination was slightly more effective than a programme emphasizing motor coordination in training Head Start children to copy the patterns of the Rutgers Test. Although she used this test as an indicator of general 'readiness', she admits that her findings can only have specific relevance for a pattern-copying task.

The programmes discussed here represent only a selection of the large number currently being published and propagated. The time seems ripe for a pause for evaluation. In general, the available evidence does not indicate that training programmes for sensory and motor organization specifically improve educational attainment. It seems likely that much of the benefit they engender results from careful grading of activities. This, in turn, enables the pupil to achieve progress which is noticeable to himself and to his teacher, and so both experience success.

Behaviour observation methods, such as those devised by the Hutts in the study mentioned earlier in this chapter, would seem to offer useful ways to evaluate the effects of sensory and motor organization programmes on behavioural adequacy.

CHAPTER 7

Sensory and Motor Organization Disabilities and Educational Adequacy

In the previous chapter the effect of disabilities in sensory and motor organization on behavioural adequacy was discussed with reference to each of the component functions. In this chapter the possible effects of these disabilities will be considered with reference to each of the basic educational attainments in turn. As always, any division of the subject matter is arbitrary. In this case, the separate consideration of reading and spelling, for example, is liable to obscure the facts that learning one is influenced by learning the other and that good teaching emphasizes their interdependence. Once again it is important to stress that the separate examination of the basic forms of educational attainment in this chapter is purely a matter of expediency.

One general point can be made about the relationship between sensory and motor organization disabilities and educational attainment. The behavioural consequences resulting from these disabilities, which were discussed in the previous chapter, are clearly likely to influence the child's ability to fit into the school routine and to benefit from teaching. Bereiter and Engelmann (1966) provide a graphic description of the way in which teaching is liable to 'flow by' distractible children. This problem is familiar to any teacher and clinician but unfortunately it is frequently not recognized as a specific disability with major handicapping consequences. Hallahan (1970) has compared the behavioural characteristics reported among deprived children in American Head Start programmes to those of 'brain-injured' children. He stresses the extent to which these children's distractibility and impulsive response in discrimination tasks handicaps them in their response to schooling. Zucker and Stricker (1968) demonstrated some of these handicaps in disadvantaged children using some of Kagan's measures of impulsivity. Klaus and Gray (1968) included training in auditory and visual discrimination as a means of establishing appropriate selective attention in their programme for disadvantaged pre-school children.

McDill *et al.* (1969) found this programme (which of course included many additional aspects) to be one of the two most effective ones they studied. Hallahan suggests that compensatory education, based on Cruickshank's techniques for reducing distraction, might be appropriate. It seems, however, from McDill *et al.*'s evaluation of the most effective programmes, that structure and the specific direction of children's attention in normal classroom settings were the most effective components.

Reading

At first glance, one would suppose that there should be a close association between visual and auditory sensory organization and reading, since reading is concerned with visual symbols representing speech sounds. The voluminous research on this topic has, however, failed to come up with any conclusive results. There are several reasons for this.

First, both sensory organization and reading are very complex processes, but studies examining their association have often made insufficient allowance for this. The number of different components of sensory and motor organization has already been emphasized but it will be necessary briefly to look at the component functions of reading.

Second, research on this problem has often been started from the wrong end. Studies comparing good and poor readers are an example of this. It is evident that reading attainment is the consequence of a large number of factors and of their interaction over a period of time. Disabilities in sensory organization, if relevant at all, are likely to constitute only one group of contributory factors. A more appropriate research strategy would be to compare the reading attainment of groups of children selected for their good or poor sensory organization in the first place.

Such a strategy is normally used in the research design of studies investigating reading readiness. In these, typically, a group of tests is given to children at the start of schooling and their scores on the variables investigated are then compared with their educational achievement at later stages in schooling. These studies have, however, also failed to provide conclusive results. One of the main reasons for this is that the research design appears to assume that quality of teaching is irrelevant to the progress children make. This is illustrated by a common finding in these studies—namely, that while children who score highly on readiness tests tend subsequently to make good progress, the prediction for children who score poorly is less reliable (Wedell 1971). Presumably a proportion of these low-scoring children do well if they are taught well, and badly if they are taught badly.

It is, of course, easy to criticize research. Rather than regret the absence of conclusive results, one would do better to accept the inconclusive findings as themselves offering proof of the complexity of the relationship between sensory organization and reading.

Reading is concerned with language. In reading, the individual 'decodes' a set of symbols into a language with which he is (hopefully) familiar. His facility with language consequently plays a very determining role in the success of his decoding. Belmont and Birch (1966), for example, matched average and poor readers (boys aged nine to ten) on class placement, age and Full-Scale IQ on the Wechsler Intelligence Scale for Children. They found that the poorer readers were relatively poorer on the verbal than on the performance scales of the WISC.

Goodman (1968) emphasizes the importance of language facility in reading competence. He points out that in the early stages of reading the child is concerned in visually discriminating letters, letter patterns or word shapes. What particular units he uses in his cue selection will depend on his skill in reading, and on whether he has been taught by a look-and-say or phonic approach. These units then have to be decoded into phonemes (sounds), phoneme patterns or whole words. If the child has decoded into phonemes or phoneme patterns, he has to blend these in order to arrive at a sound pattern which he can recognize as a word. He may have to try several alternate blendings before he achieves this. It is only at this point that he can derive meaning from what he reads. The analysis illustrates in this way how a child may bark at print without understanding it. With increasing proficiency the reader progressively telescopes the middle stages, until he can derive meaning directly from print.

A particularly important stage of Goodman's analysis is his postulated recoding of the sound patterns derived from the graphemes (written symbols, letters). At this stage there is clearly much scope for extrapolation for the child who is verbally fluent. Not only is he more likely to be able to guess a word from fewer sound cues, but his familiarity with syntax will enable him to extrapolate word endings and even auxiliary verbs and other parts of sentences. If, in addition, he understands what he is reading and the passage is fairly simple, he will be able correctly to guess even complete words. This type of reader is well known to most teachers, because he often tries his luck too far, and makes errors (like reading 'boat' for 'ship'). Analysis of the errors usually confirms that these are not random. Verb endings, for example, tend not to be added to nouns. The extent to which a knowledge of syntactical, grammatical and grapheme-phoneme association rules help the average reader, is shown by the ease with which nonsense passages conforming to these rules can be pronounced and understood. Lewis Carroll's famous poem, 'The Jabberwocky' illustrates this point and Goodman analyses an illustrative example of his own. The reader may like to prove the point for himself by reading the following limerick and by answering the questions which follow. The reader will find that he is quite able to make up sentences using the nonsense words in answering the questions.

> There was a bild quiffle of Snode,
> Who beglayed like a drantle of frode.
> 'Crive me a shum cleast
> And I will be meefed,'
> Blathed crenchly that quiffle of Snode.

Questions:

1   How did the quiffle beglay?
2(a) What did the quiffle blathe?
 (b) How did he blathe?
3   What kind of cleast did the quiffle wish to have criven?

An individual's dependence on sensory organization in reading is thus relative to his skill in extrapolation, which, in turn, is related to the predictability of his reading matter. These considerations in themselves can already be seen to make the relationship between sensory organization and reading achievement complex. It is evident that sensory organization is more critical in the early stages of reading than later on.

Visual sensory organization

Gibson (1965) points out that reading involves, as a first step, the visual discrimination of letter and word configurations. The question arises, however, whether this can be achieved by skill in visual discrimination in general, or whether it involves skill in making particular kinds of discrimination. T. C. Barrett (1965) reviewed research relating first-grade reading achievement to pre-reading visual discrimination. He concluded that a closer association was found when the measures of visual discrimination involved literal material (letters, letter-like shapes and words) than non-literal material (such as abstract patterns). De Hirsch *et al.* (1966) show data with similar implications in their study. They gave thirty-seven tests to a sample of kindergarten children, and correlated the scores on these with the children's scores on three measures of educational attainment when they reached second grade. These measures consisted of a composite reading score derived from tests of silent and oral reading, a spelling test, and an evaluation of the children's handwriting in the spelling test. The correlations tended to be higher for girls than for boys. The correlation coefficients for the whole sample showed a significant relationship between reading and a word-matching test but not between reading and a figure-ground discrimination test. Such findings could, of course, be taken to indicate that the children who were already familiar with letter and word shapes in kindergarten would be more likely to succeed at reading later—not a very startling conclusion. The finding is, however, important, since it suggests that children need to be able not only to discriminate but also to know *what* to discriminate. Rosen (1966), for example, gave an adapted version of the Frostig programme to a random sample of first-grade children for twenty-nine half-hour daily sessions. These sessions overlapped for a quarter of an hour with the time normally allotted to daily reading instruction. Rosen compared the children's reading progress with that of a group of first-grade children who were given a quarter of an hour additional reading instruction daily. When the individual differences in the children's initial scores on the Frostig and Metropolitan reading readiness tests at the start of the first grade were held constant, the group receiving perceptual training was not found to have made significantly more progress.

In the context of the present discussion, the experimental group represented children who were improving in sensory organization skills, but were getting less instruction in applying this to reading. The control group children, presumably, were getting more instruction in applying their sensory organization to reading.

There is some indication from the study of Gibson *et al.* (1962) cited in Chapter 3 that children between four and eight make particular progress in the discrimination of visuo-spatial dimensions which are relevant to reading and writing. This experiment showed that children made particular progress in orientation and line-to-curve discrimination, although they were not reported to have had any specific perceptual training. These findings emphasize that learning reading and writing itself involves visual discrimination training. It is likely, however, that the capacity to discriminate the relevant features of a visual display itself depends on certain components of sensory organization. Goins (1958), for example, inferred from a study in which she gave children fourteen perceptual tests at the beginning of first grade, that the tests which predicted reading achievement at the end of first grade most accurately had a high loading on a factor analogous to Thurstone's (1944) 'flexibility' factor. Goins describes this factor as 'the ability to keep in mind a figure against distraction'. In the context of the model of sensory organization used in this book, this would seem to be an aspect of the interaction between cue selection and analysis. The importance of flexibility in the interaction between 'cue selection' and 'analysis' has already been stressed. Morris (1966) reports a finding which may be relevant to this. She found that the poor readers in her study reported that they remembered words more consistently on the basis of *either* whole word shape *or* word part. Good readers, on the other hand, tended to vary their approach. Maslow *et al.* (1964) report a small study in which a group of kindergarten children were given the Frostig test in July of one year and their reading progress followed up in October of the same year. Although the children had been exposed to pre-reading and reading materials on a demand basis since the previous May, Maslow *et al.* report that none of the children obtaining a perceptual quotient below 90 had begun to read by October (although a child with a PQ of 122 had failed to start). The authors do not, however, indicate which of the skills involved in the five subtests appeared to be limiting the children's progress.

Several researchers have indicated that children rapidly develop specific skills in selective attention to parts of words. Marchbanks and Levin (1965) report a study in which kindergarten and first-grade children were required to discriminate 'pseudo-words' visually. Given a particular pseudo-word they had to find a match for it in a multiple-choice series which contained distractor words of the same length and included one letter from the stimulus word. The authors found that in three-letter words children matched mainly on the basis of the first letters. Final letters were used next most frequently, but less so in five-letter words than in three-letter words. The research data did not indicate that word shape played a significant role in word matching.

Gibson *et al.* (1963) report a study in which they found that children in first grade were already beginning to build up expectations about the combinations in which letters were likely to occur in words. Gibson made up lists of three-letter 'pronounceable' and three-letter 'unpronounceable' pseudo-words (e.g. NAR and RNA), and compared children's ability to spell these out when they were briefly exposed in a tachistoscope. They also presented lists of real words made up of the same letters (e.g. RAN). The results showed that the first-graders spelt out real words best, but also spelt the 'pronounceable' pseudo-words better than the 'unpronounceable' ones. Vernon (1971) cites a study by Thomas which cast some doubt on whether the pronounceability of the trigrams was the factor determining their recognition.

Findings such as these show that the skills involved in the visual perception of words become specialized very rapidly. Presumably, progress in reading depends on this kind of specialization and this explains why many studies have found that correlations between performance on non-literal visual discrimination tests and reading tend to decrease, the higher the age at which these two performances are compared (see, for example, Gates 1922, 1926, quoted in Vernon 1971). This does not, of course, necessarily limit the predictive value of pre-school tests of visual discrimination. If visual discrimination is one of the necessary prerequisites for learning to read, then early readers are likely to discriminate adequately, and also to be in a better position to make subsequent progress, because of their earlier start in reading (Durkin 1969). None the less, it must be stressed that the moderate correlation coefficients of predictive studies allow for the proviso 'other things being equal'. B. K. Keogh and C. E. Smith (1967), for example, found significant correlations between performance on the Bender Gestalt Test given to children at kindergarten age, and these children's reading scores on the Iowa Test of Basic Skills at sixth grade. Analysis of the children's scores indicated that Bender scores were predictive of both high and low reading achievement. The significance of Keogh and Smith's findings will be considered again below.

Language facility is also likely to help children to learn to discriminate those visual features relevant to reading. Luria's work (1961) has shown the way in which visual discrimination can be aided by verbal formulation as was pointed out in Chapter 3. Diack (1960) mentions an anecdote about a little girl aged two, who was fond of jelly. When presented with the capital letters of the alphabet on separate cards, she was unable to match them. When told the 'J' stood for jelly she was immediately able to match the 'J's. Clearly language can help a great deal in providing meaningful associations for the visual discrimination involved in learning to read.

One of the most frequently found types of error in the visual discrimination of words is the confusion of letters and words and their reversals. In the case of words, the error usually involves transposition rather than reversal of letters (as in 'saw' for 'was'). It was noted in the previous chapter that children had difficulty in the discrimination of the left–right orientation of shapes. It has been argued that, when children learn the constancy of an object in their environment, they have to learn that it remains the same object, whatever its orientation. Learning to distinguish 'd's and 'b's consequently involves unlearning such an acquired generalization. Such an argument can only partly apply, since learning about the use of objects such as a cup must clearly involve discriminating whether it is the right way up. The discrimination of reversals was one of the dimensions which Gibson found to improve in her study of four- to eight-year-old children. The good reader, presumably, also learns to identify letters on the basis of their association with a particular word. For example, with increasing experience of words in his reading, he knows that 'bat' is a more probable combination than 'dat'.

Transposition of letters in words was found by Morris (1966) to be the most common type of error made by poor readers. It has sometimes been proposed that this type of error results from defective eye movements. Bond and Tinker (1967) point out that poor eye movements in reading are much more likely to be the result of poor reading. When a child is uncertain of what he is reading, he is more likely to use a to-and-fro eye-scanning movement in his search for some words or letters that he recognizes. 'Regressive' eye movements are more frequently found among poor readers, as was stated in Chapter 5. This is just one more example of the vicious circle of accumulated difficulties faced by the poor reader. Fernald (1943) and Cruickshank *et al.* (1961) both advocate the integration of reading and writing instruction to help the child overcome these confusions about word orientation.

Auditory sensory organization

Duration in time is an inherent characteristic of auditory stimuli, and this presents a major contrast to visual stimuli. The transient nature of sounds obliges the individual to rely partly on his auditory memory in most types of auditory discrimination. For example, if the child is asked to discriminate the words 'tap' and 'tab' when they are written down, he can look from one to the other in any sequence and for as long as he pleases. But if he has to distinguish between the words when they are uttered, he has to rely on his memory. In order to help himself over the difficulty of remembering the word sounds, a child—and even the adult—will frequently repeat them to himself orally. Discrimination then is likely not only to depend on the individual's auditory memory, but also on his articulation skills. In Goodman's model of the reading process, auditory discrimination is involved when the child builds up the phonemes associated with the letters or letter groups in a word and matches these with the sounds of words in his own aural vocabulary. Teachers are familiar with the way in which this sound 'blending' often involves vocal or subvocal articulation, and this may account for Bannatyne and Wichiarajote's (1969) and Wepman's (1960) findings that articulation skills were correlated with reading achievement.

The study of the association between auditory discrimination and reading has usually been concerned with speech sounds or with rhythm. Stambak (1951), for example, found that poor readers were worse at reproducing a sequence of tapped-out rhythms. De Hirsch *et al.* (1966) found that kindergarten children's level of performance in copying rhythmic taps was predictive of their subsequent reading attainment at second grade. Tansley (1967) and Barry (1961) include rhythmic tapping exercises in their remedial programmes, but the effectiveness of these components has not been evaluated.

The discrimination of speech sounds has been studied with the following range of tasks:

(a) Discrimination of words and nonsense syllables varying in vowels, consonants, etc. (for example, Wepman 1958).

(*b*) Recognition of words when the constituent sounds are either individually articulated or only partly given (for example, Kirk *et al.* 1968).

(*c*) Identification of one sound in a polysyllabic word, or repetition of a part of a word (for example, Rosner and Simon 1971).

Such tasks clearly measure the extent to which the child is aware of the constituent sounds and sound groupings of his language. This, in turn, is essential if the child is to learn to apply the grapheme-phoneme code when he is taught reading 'phonically'. It is not surprising therefore, that Dykstra (1966) found that studies investigating the association of auditory discrimination and reading revealed higher correlations where children had been taught reading with a phonic emphasis. Chall (1967) concluded from her survey of methods of teaching reading that phonic methods were more effective, and so auditory discrimination can be seen as an important function in reading acquisition, and even more in reading progress. Dykstra in his review of research found that poor readers were generally reported to be poorer in auditory discrimination tasks. Bateman (1967) found better auditory memory among good readers. She also investigated the effectiveness of matching teaching method to individual differences in auditory and visual memory among children. She selected two groups of first-grade children, one whose performance on the Auditory Sequencing subtest of the ITPA was better than that on the Visual Sequencing subtest and another group with the opposite pattern of skills. Each group of children was then given reading instruction with a 'phonic' or 'look-and-say' emphasis, according to their relative levels of visual and auditory memory. Bateman did not find that children taught along these lines made more progress than control groups of children whose reading instruction was not matched to their relative strengths and weaknesses.

It is not certain, however, that these findings can be taken as conclusive evidence on this issue. It is difficult to be certain that the ITPA subtests were performed by the children with the particular functions the tests were assumed to measure: for example, children sometimes help themselves by naming the patterns in the series which they are expected to remember visually in the Visual Sequencing Test. Analogously, it is difficult to be certain that reading instruction for each group was kept 'pure', as Bateman herself admits. The children in Bateman's groups were all of well above general ability and, as has already been implied, such children are more likely to be able to compensate for any one particular area of weakness.

Most teachers of reading probably use a combination of 'look-and-say' and 'phonic' approaches but change from an emphasis on the former to an emphasis on the latter as children progress. It is possible that reading failure is sometimes due to the fact that an individual child's sensory organization does not develop in line with the change in emphasis from 'visual' to 'phonic' methods. A child with visual discrimination disability may be unable to benefit from a look-and-say approach at the time that this is being used. By the time his visual discrimination improves, either in the course of development or through remedial training, his class is likely to have reached the stage where phonics are introduced and so the child is not helped to learn to apply his newly developed visual discrimination skills to reading. In this kind of situation a child may fail to learn to apply his discrimination skills because his development is 'out of step' with the teaching sequence to which he is exposed.

Intersensory integration

Several researchers (Birch and Belmont 1965, Stambak 1951) have been interested in the association between visual and auditory stimuli, since they regard this as one of the functions underlying reading ability. They have studied this by asking children to identify visual patterns representing rhythmic patterns. In Birch and Belmont's study, the experimenter tapped out a rhythm and presented the child with groups of dots and dashes, one of which corresponded to the pattern tapped. Birch and Belmont found that a group of children with reading disability were poorer at this task than a control group. One may ask, however, whether this task was anything more than a form of auditory-visual coding. In some senses, clearly, any intersensory association involves coding of one set of sensory stimuli in terms of another. However, the coding in Birch and Belmont's task is clearly very different even from the association involved, for example, in their tactile-kinesthetic association task (see Chapter 3). One is familiar with the child who, when asked to represent a rhythmic pattern with pencil and paper, draws a series of equidistant vertical lines corresponding in number to the beats of the rhythm. The rhythm itself is represented by the time intervals between drawing each line. The 'coding' in Birch and Belmont's task is clearly more complex and involves representing temporal duration by spatial distance. They did not find that their reading disability group's low performance resulted only from difficulty in the analysis of sound sequences. It seems possible that the difficulty lies in the simultaneous carrying out of two analyses—that of the auditory sequence and that of the visual displays. Stambak found that, although 66 per cent of her reading disability group had mastered the principle of her auditory-visual association task (which was similar to Birch and Belmont's) by nine years, none of them were able to apply it. This contrasted with her control group, all of whom had mastered the principle by nine years, and were able to apply it by ten years. This difficulty in simultaneous analysis may arise from the fact that neither of the processes of analysis is sufficiently mastered. The individual attention each analysis requires may preclude the effective association of the two.

Whether or not this account of the problems involved in Birch and Belmont's and Stambak's tasks is correct, it nonetheless seems true that their tasks are better described as involving the application of a set of conventions. Similarly, the auditory-visual association involved in reading should be classed as an analogous problem.

General comments

This discussion of sensory organization and reading has shown how the child may approach the task of reading with different skills at different stages of mastery. His approach will also vary according to the familiarity of the material he is reading, and even according to the nature of the words used (for example whether they are phonically regular or not). His success in the task depends not only on the flexibility with which he can switch from one approach to the other, but also on the 'flexibility' of his sensory organization of visual and auditory stimuli. Of most importance, however, is the child's facility in language.

It is evident that sensory organization quickly becomes specialized in reading both through the child's own practice and through the teaching he receives. The child with limited levels of sensory organization may find these to be sufficient, so long as he is taught how to use them, and so long as his language facility is also adequate. However, if these supportive factors are not available to the child, sensory organization skills may well become more essential to him. This compensatory principle in the achievement of educational adequacy has been brought out by B. K. Keogh (1971).

Spelling

The term 'spelling' refers to a variety of activities, including the following:

(*a*) Uttering the names or sounds of the letters in a word either: (1) spontaneously or (2) in response to the utterance of the word (for example, by the teacher).
(*b*) Writing a word either (1) spontaneously or (2) to dictation. Both of these activities may involve writing the word in isolation or in a passage.

These activities are clearly very diverse. This section will be primarily concerned with spelling, in sense (*b*) above.

In contrast to reading, spelling may be called an 'encoding' task. The child is assumed to know what he wants to say and now has to encode the phonemes of the relevant words into graphemes and grapheme groups. Just as in reading, the units used in encoding may range from sentences to individual sounds. In contrast to reading, however, the child has no scope for extrapolation—he cannot leave out words or parts of words, but has to complete each detail of the code to achieve acceptable spelling. Such encoding may include 'saying the word to oneself' (that is, vocal or subvocal articulation) as an aid to auditory analysis. When the word is written down, the child, if he is uncertain, will tend to check it. This may involve checking the familiarity of the 'feel' of writing the word (that is, kinesthetic memory) or checking the 'look of the word' (that is, visual memory). Alternatively, the graphemes may be decoded back into the relevant phonemes and so checked against the child's memory of the sound of the word. This may be done with or without articulating the word. Furthermore, what has been written down may be checked against familiar rules such as 'i before e, except after c'.

From the above, it is evident that spelling involves a wide variety of functions, both in originally writing down a word, and in checking it. The same skills may not be used in writing and in checking a word, and different skills may be used for familiar and for unfamiliar words. Indeed, different skills may be used in the same word. For example, the word 'station' may be written from the encoding of the sounds s-t-a, and from the memory of the spelling rule for the sound 'shun'.

Predictive studies relating sensory organization to spelling achievement have been carried out by De Hirsch et al. (1966) and by B. K. Keogh and C. E. Smith (1967). As in reading, spelling achievement was found to be associated with visual discrimination of letter rather than non-literal shapes. De Hirsch et al. found a non-significant correlation between visual figure-ground discrimination at kindergarten level and spelling at second grade, in contrast to significant correlations for the Gates word-matching test and for the Horst Reversal Test. Performance on the Wepman auditory discrimination test and on the memory for tapped rhythms were also significantly correlated. The rhythm memory test is the only one not directly involving language or language symbols. It is evident that in spelling also, sensory organization becomes relevant in so far as it is applied to the specific task.

The association which Keogh and Smith and also de Hirsch et al. found between performance on the Bender test (Koppitz scoring) in kindergarten children and later achievement in spelling cannot, however, be explained in the above terms. The shapes of the Bender test have only a limited similarity to letters. However, the Koppitz scoring criteria were originally validated against classroom achievement. One can only assume that the correlations which Keogh and Smith found were due to the kinds of discrimination and to the aspects of performance which the scoring system assesses, rather than to the characteristics of the patterns themselves. Furthermore, as we found with reading, well-developed sensory and motor organization is likely to help the child in the initial acquisition of spelling and this initial advantage in spelling is itself likely to foster further progress. While one might, therefore, postulate a direct causal relationship when the child is starting to spell, the causal relationship subsequently becomes indirect.

An analysis of the component skills of spelling using a comparison of good and poor spellers was carried out by Bannatyne and Wichiarajote (1969). They compared children with higher and lower spelling scores in third-grade classes—in other words, children who had already been exposed to spelling for some time. On the basis of their findings, Bannatyne and Wichiarajote found that motor organization was a major component of spelling performance. They associated this with the articulatory processes involved in sound blending and particularly with the formation of sounds in their correct sequence.

In the introduction to this chapter it was suggested that the effect of sensory and motor organization on achievement was best studied by contrasting the educational performance of children distinguished on the basis of their level of sensory and motor organization in the first place. Day and Wedell (1972) designed their investigation of the role of auditory and visual memory in spelling along these lines. They gave the ITPA Visual-motor Sequencing subtest and the Stambak Memory for Rhythms test to 140 children aged eight to ten in ordinary schools. From among these children, they selected three groups on the basis of their standard scores on the tests. Group A consisted of twenty-two children whose performance on the auditory memory test was markedly better than on the visual memory test. Group B contained eighteen children whose scores on the visual memory test were markedly better than on the auditory memory test. Group C consisted of twenty-one children whose scores on both tests differed by standard scores of less than 0·16 (see Table 7.1).

Table 7.1

	Group A $N=22$	Group B $N=18$	Group C $N=21$
ITPA Visual-motor Sequencing Test: mean scores (range in parentheses)	10·18 (5–13)	15·83 (12–24)	13·76 (4–19)
Stambak *Reproduction de Structures Rythmiques Test*: mean scores (range in parentheses)	15·00 (11–17)	9·94 (3–18)	13·52 (5–18)
Schonell spelling test of irregular words: mean scores	22·64	20·50	24·24

Data from a study of visual and auditory memory and spelling. (From Day, J., and Wedell, K. (1972), Visual and auditory memory in spelling, *British Journal of Educational Psychology*, **42**, pp. 33–9 and reproduced by permission)

The memory tests were chosen because they did not involve speech sounds or verbal symbols, and because both tests involved the discrimination of elements in sequence. The children in the three selected groups were given the Schonell irregular word spelling test 1A (F. J. Schonell 1932), and no significant differences in mean spelling scores were found between the groups. The conclusions drawn from this finding were analogous to those stated above about reading. First, children approach a task such as spelling with whatever skills they possess, compensating for their less well developed skills by their better developed skills. Second, the absolute level of a particular component skill is not so critical as the relative levels of all the component skills. For example, group C's mean scores on the memory tasks were only average and yet, in rank order, its mean spelling score was the highest. However, its scores were average on *both* memory tasks and this was, no doubt, the significant point.

The absence of significant differences between the groups' spelling scores might have been taken to indicate that the memory tasks did not, in fact, represent relevant component skills. However, it was found that there were differences in the types of error made by the three groups. Each child had been allowed to continue with the spelling test until he made ten errors, and these errors were then categorized according to the classification proposed by Livingston (1961). Because it is difficult to avoid subjectivity in such classifications, errors were termed 'unclassifiable' unless they fell clearly within one of Livingston's categories. Almost 25 per cent of the errors were regarded as unclassifiable, and group C made significantly fewer of these than the other two groups. The small proportion of unclassifiable errors found in group C suggested that these children, being less able to depend on superior auditory and visual memory, depended more on the application of spelling rules to achieve their performance in spelling.

Group A, who scored particularly highly on the auditory memory task, made significantly fewer errors involving confusion of syllables. This error category refers, for example, to the inclusion of a wrong sound in a word (as in 'sitowated' for 'situated'). Both group A and group B had a poorer grasp of phoneme-grapheme associations than group C, but group A appear to have been able to use their more acute auditory memory in spelling.

Group B demonstrated their better visual memory by making fewer 'one-for-two' doubling errors (as in 'mery' for 'merry') and fewer omissions of single letters (as in 'engin' for 'engine'). However, these differences did not quite reach statistical significance.

Corresponding differences in types of error made were also apparent when the most frequent wrongly spelt words in each group were compared.

For example, the following were the unsuccessful attempts made to spell the word 'hardly' by children in groups A and B.

Group A	Group B
hardley	hardley
hardl	harle
hardy	harlde
hadly	hargle
hadten	hrard
heady	hrge
	hain
	hoewlind
	doneley
	fedle

On a subjective evaluation of these misspellings, it seems that children in Group A made a better attempt at preserving the syllabic rhythm and consonant structure of the words.

The fact that children seemed to tackle spelling with whatever skills they have available may also have disadvantageous aspects. The fact that both groups A and B made more unclassifiable errors suggests that they came to rely too much on their respective strong areas of memory, and paid less attention to learning spelling rules.

The findings of this study suggest that the qualitative aspects of performance on a particular educational task must be considered if the effect of component skills is to be identified since they cannot adequately be distinguished by differences in aggregate scores.

Evidence that children differ in their approach to a spelling task also comes from a study by Peters (1967). She compared the types of spelling error made by eight-year-old children who had been taught reading by the 'look-and-say' method with those made by children taught with an emphasis on phonics (using the initial teaching alphabet). She found that there was a difference between the predominance of different types of error in each group. The look-and-say children produced fewer homophones and errors of doubling and substitution of consonants, in contrast to the 'phonic' children, who made fewest transpositions and vowel substitutions. The total number of errors made by the children in each group was very similar. Each of these teaching methods thus appears to have induced a particular approach to spelling in their respective groups of children. Peters' study illustrates how teaching may influence a child's cue selection, and that this, in turn, is reflected in the stimulus dimensions he remembers. Peters subdivided her groups further, into those children with IQs between 85 and

115 and those with IQs above this level. She found that the significant differences between error categories were confined to the lower IQ group. It might well be argued that the absence of error differences among the children of superior intelligence was due to the fact that they were not dependent on the teacher for acquiring spelling skills in the first place. Bright children might be more able to infer 'spelling patterns' (in Gibson's sense) regardless of the method by which they were taught. However, Peters' findings do not provide clear evidence on this, since the bright children appear to have made too few errors in most categories to show a difference.

The influence of a knowledge of spelling rules, or of 'spelling patterns' as Gibson describes them, is illustrated in a study by Chapman *et al.* (1970). They included an analysis of transposition errors in simple one-syllable words in their study of children aged 7½ to 8½. These children were asked to spell some of the words from Daniels and Diack's 'reversible words' subtest of the Standard Reading Test Battery. Relatively few of the 150 children made transposition errors. Transposition errors were defined as words in which the correct letters were written in the wrong order (as in 'but' for 'tub'). Only eighteen such errors were in fact made by the 150 children, but in only one of these words was the vowel transposed to the end of the word ('saw' was spelt 'swa'). Five children, by comparison, spelt 'saw' as 'was'. The one transposition error of the vowel was the only relatively 'unpronounceable' word produced among the children's transposition errors.

Bateman (1967) also investigated spelling achievement in her study on the effects of matching method of teaching reading to children's relative scores on the Auditory and Visual Sequencing subtests of the ITPA. She did not find any evidence that matching teaching method to children's 'strengths' or 'weaknesses' in these types of memory affected their gains on a spelling task. These results have to be considered in the light of the qualifications previously mentioned. Peters' finding that differences in method of teaching reading were not reflected in the spelling errors of the children with above-average abilities in her study, perhaps also accounts for Bateman's negative results.

M. Murphy and M. McHugh (1971) studied the effects of matching method of remedial teaching in spelling to ESN children with contrasting scores on the 'visual' and 'auditory' subtests of the ITPA. They found a statistically significant interaction between teaching method and the children's *better* perceptual skills. The children whom they regarded as 'auditorily' handicapped made better progress when taught by a visual method and the children regarded as having a visual handicap did better when taught by an auditory method. Murphy and McHugh's children were older than Bateman's, and also were of considerably lower general abilities.

The levels of spelling skill investigated may not, however, have been so different. The contrast between the findings of these two studies emphasizes again the need to take into consideration the compensatory interaction of children's abilities.

These divergent research findings present a confusing picture. However, when one remembers the complexity of the spelling task as set out at the beginning of this section, one can hardly be surprised. The research findings refer to children with different patterns of abilities, at different stages of spelling, performing on different types of spelling task, after different types of instruction. What does emerge is that visual sensory organization and visual memory help the child to deal with the irregularities of English spelling. Auditory sensory organization and memory, and the motor organization involved in articulation, help the child to build up unfamiliar words. It appears that disabilities in any one of these functions have a handicapping effect only if they are very severe, or if they involve several functions and if the child does not have the reasoning capacity to assimilate spelling rules.

Handwriting

The role of the various sensory and motor organization functions involved in handwriting is likely to vary according to the way handwriting is taught, and to whether it is taught at all. If the child is taught handwriting, there is likely to be, from the start, an emphasis on hand and arm movement patterns. While the child is required to reproduce a letter or some partial letter shape, and thus will have to learn to attend to selected visual dimensions (size, curvature, etc.), he is also encouraged to attend to the 'feel' of the movements he is making—to kinesthetic feedback. Sometimes, at this early stage, visual 'monitoring' of movement is expressly avoided; the child is asked to make the required movements with his eyes shut so that he can direct his attention to the 'feel' of his movements. This approach to the learning of handwriting is aimed at building up short movement sequences, which can then be incorporated as units into longer movement sequences in the hierarchical organization of movement described earlier. When a child, taught in this way, is asked to 'copy' a word or sentence, he will tend to 'represent' rather than reproduce what he is asked to copy. He will write out the word or sentence he is required to copy by reproducing the letter shapes in the style which he has been taught, and he will probably only 'copy' the actual letter sequence.

The child who is not taught handwriting will, by contrast, be much more concerned with the visual discrimination of letter shapes. For him, copying a word or sentence will, in the initial stages, be analogous to copying a pattern. He will construct his 'patterns' as best he can, with whatever movements he finds necessary. Children referred for handwriting problems sometimes show indications that they started to write in this way and were not able to solve the problems involved on their own. They may form letters from the bottom upwards, or with more strokes than are necessary. For example, children may make an 's' with a separate stroke for each of the curves.

Most research on handwriting has been concerned with comparing the efficiency of different styles of handwriting. Relatively few studies have been concerned with investigating children's handwriting difficulties, although these are increasingly being mentioned in studies of children with learning disabilities. A major problem in studying children's handwriting difficulties has been to devise an objective means of assessment. Various matching-to-sample methods have been proposed, but none is very satisfactory.

Brenner and Gillman (1966) mention handwriting difficulties as common among their group of children with specific perceptuo-motor difficulties. Adams (1969) reports a pilot study in which 79 per cent of a group of eighty-four educationally handicapped children were reported to have difficulty in writing as well as in reading and spelling. Chapman et al. (1970) reported that approximately 12 per cent of boys, and 5 per cent of girls aged $7\frac{1}{2}$ to $8\frac{1}{2}$, in a random sample of children in ordinary schools were unable to write recognizably one or more of ten letters. (This study will be reported in greater detail below.)

A few studies have investigated the sensory and motor organization involved in handwriting. De Hirsch et al. (1966) included an assessment of handwriting in their follow-up study of kindergarten children. They found a significant correlation between scores on the Bender test at kindergarten age and handwriting at second grade. Tests of visual discrimination, however, were not found to be predictive of handwriting. Similarly, H. R. Lewis and H. P. Lewis (1964) found no correlation between first-grade children's scores on the matching subtest of the Metropolitan reading test and the standard of their handwriting. Wedell and Horne (1969) followed up the first-year infant children whose sensory and motor organization skills they had investigated (see Chapter 6). When the children were in their final term at infant school, they were given the sentence in subtest 3 of the Daniels and Diack battery to copy (Daniels and Diack 1970). Three teachers were then asked to rank the children's handwriting in this task. The ten lowest-ranking children were all in the group which had the worst performance on the motor organization task (plasticine model copying) eighteen months earlier. Four of these children had also scored poorly on the visual discrimination task, but none of the children had scored poorly on the eye-hand coordination task. By contrast none of the children who scored above a cut-off score on the plasticine copying task and on the

Bender test eighteen months earlier obtained a low ranking on the sentence-copying task. Figure 7.1 shows examples of the performance of children with good and with poor handwriting on the pattern-copying and tracing tasks.

It appears, then, that motor organization disability rather than poor visual discrimination is the main dysfunction underlying poor handwriting. On the other hand, it does appear that intensive instruction can help a child with motor organization difficulties to write adequately. One child in Wedell and Horne's study who made relatively low scores on the plasticine copying task when tested in his first year at infant school, was ranked fifth out of thirty-nine in the sentence-copying task eighteen months later.

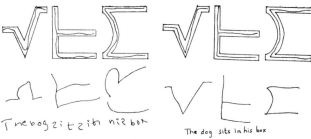

Figure 7.1. Tracing and handwriting of six-year-old children with poor and good performance on pattern copying. (From Wedell, K. (1968), Perceptual-motor difficulties, *Special Education*, **57** (4), p. 25–30 by permission of The Spastics Society and Association for Special Education)

As mentioned above, deciding on criteria for assessing handwriting presents one of the main difficulties in carrying out research on this aspect of educational attainment. Wedell and Horne sidestepped the issue by using experienced teachers' evaluations. It was interesting to note that there was considerable agreement among the three teachers although no formal criteria were drawn up. In general, the teachers seemed to be considering aspects such as letter shape, proportion, relative position of adjacent letters, and grouping of letters in words. Lines and Widlake (1971) report a detailed study of handwriting errors in a small sample of socially deprived six- to seven-year-old children, amongst whom the main types of error were found to involve the relative size, shape and position of letters. Gross errors of letter shape were rarer. The handwriting assessment was based on children's performance on the 'copying a sentence' subtest of the Daniels and Diack Standard Reading Test Battery.

Incorrect orientation of letters is one of the most frequently found types of errors. To some extent this has to be seen as a residual difficulty, since an error can only be classed as an orientation error if it is sufficiently well formed to be recognizable as such. F. J. Schonell (1948) found that letter reversals tended normally to disappear from children's handwriting at about eight years of age—slightly earlier than in reading. He found that girls ceased to make reversals earlier than boys. Chapman *et al.* (1970) found a similar difference between boys and girls in their study of 328 children between $7\frac{1}{2}$ and $8\frac{1}{2}$ years of age. The children were required to write ten 'reversible' lower-case letters and seven 'reversible' numbers to dictation. A considerable minority of children were still found to make orientation errors, as can be seen in Table 7.2. Chapman *et al.* classified the orientation

Table 7.2

Percentages of subjects making different numbers of errors

	Letters				Digits			
	Rotations		Wrong		Rotations		Wrong	
	Boys	Girls	Boys	Girls	Boys	Girls	Boys	Girls
N	177	151	177	151	177	151	177	151
1	24·86	15·23	9·60	3·31	15·25	4·64	0·0	0·66
2	7·34	6·62	1·13	0·66	3·95	3·31	1·69	0·0
3 or more	3·39	1·98	1·69	0·66	2·82	2·65	0·0	0·0
1 or more	35·59	23·83	12·42	4·63	22·02	10·60	1·69	0·66
1 or more (adjusted)	24·91	16·69	9·09	3·24				

Percentages of eight-year-old children making different numbers of errors on letter- and digit-writing tasks (adjusted percentages in bottom line on letter-copying data). From Chapman, J. *et al.* (1970). A note on reversals in the writing of eight-year-old children, *Remedial Education*, **5**, pp. 91–94 and reproduced by permission

errors according to whether they were vertical rotation errors (as in d for b), horizontal rotation errors (as in b for p) or depth axis rotation errors (as in d for p). All except a very small proportion of rotation errors were vertical axis rotations (that is, reversals). This finding is similar to that found for pattern copying in Chapter 6, where reversal errors were found more frequently than inversion errors.

The most frequently rotated letters and digits were, not surprisingly, those which represented another letter or digit in the alternative position (as in d,9). This indicates that a child's uncertainty about the orientation of a letter is reduced when the letter has a meaningful association in only one orientation.

What are some of the factors leading some children to have greater uncertainty about letter orientation? Many opinions are held about this question, and Chapman and Wedell (1972) set out to investigate some of them. From among the children in the previously reported study, two sub-groups of children were selected—a group who made rotation or trans-position errors in at least three out of five letter- and digit-writing tasks (the R group) and a group who made none of these errors on any of the tasks (NR group). The children in the two groups were matched for age, sex, school class and scores on a verbal ability test (English picture vocabu-lary test—Brimer and Dunn 1963). The children in both groups were then given tests in the kinds of areas commonly thought to be associated with reversal errors (such as left–right discrimination, visual perception and lateral dominance). The tests and the children's mean scores are set out in Table 7.3. The mean scores of the R and NR groups were significantly

Table 7.3

	Reversers Mean	SD	Non-reversers Mean	SD	Maximum score	Significance of difference (P)
Frostig test. PQ	87	10·5	93	9·3	—	<0·02
Subtests (scaled scores)						
Eye-motor	9·3	1·0	9·9	1·4	20	NS
Figure-ground	8·0	1·4	8·4	1·7	20	NS
Constancy	8·8	2·0	9·4	1·7	20	NS
Position in Space	7·6	2·6	9·3	1·7	20	<0·05
Spatial Relationships	9·5	1·4	9·8	1·0	20	NS
Daniels and Diack subtest 4	16·1	4·1	17·0	2·0	20	NS
Benton: right–left discrimi-nation	7·2	2·6	8·5	1·9	12	NS
Kephart: 'angels-in-the-snow'	7·4	1·6	7·3	0·9	10	NS
'Crossing the mid-line'	8·3	7·5	18·2	8·4	30	<0·01
Lateral preference	No. of subjects					
Right hand, right eye	10		13	19		
Left hand, left eye	2		2	19		
Mixed and unestablished	7		4	19		

Test comparisons of reverser and non-reverser groups. (From Chapman, J., and Wedell, K. (1972), Perceptuo-motor abilities and reversal errors in children's handwriting, *J. Learning Disabilities*, **5**, pp. 321–5, by permission of Professional Press, Inc.)

different on only two of the measures of sensory and motor organization used, although the R group's scores were almost invariably lower. The R group had a lower 'perceptual quotient' on the Frostig Developmental Test of Visual Perception, and this was mainly attributable to poorer perform-ance on the orientation discrimination subtest. However, there was not a similarly marked difference between the two groups on another orientation discrimination test (subtest 4 of the Daniels and Diack standard reading battery).

The other test on which the two groups' mean scores differed significantly was an adaptation of Kephart's 'crossing the mid-line' task. Here the child is required to stand in front of a blackboard and draw a line joining two points, one to his right and one to his left. The dots are arranged diagonally and horizontally. An attempt was made to score this task objectively, by using a standard stencil, divided into five equal sections, which was placed over the child's line. The child's score was defined as the number of sections for which the child's line came within the stencil. The reversers were significantly poorer in drawing straight diagonal lines from their right to their left, and vice versa.

It was interesting to note that the two groups of children were not significantly different in their knowledge of the left and right sides of their bodies (Benton test and Kephart's 'angels in the snow' task). Nor was the lateral hand and eye preference of the groups markedly different. A tendency to make reversal errors in handwriting has often been attributed to either or both of these factors.

Before going on to speculate about the possible causes of rotation errors, three further findings need to be mentioned. The R group's mean reading and spelling scores were significantly poorer than those of the NR group (this was not attributable to differences in verbal abilities, since the two groups were matched on the English Picture Vocabulary Test). The R group's poorer spelling, but not their poorer reading, can be seen as secondary to their difficulty in handwriting.

After the children had been given the tests mentioned in Table 7.3 they were given the letter- and digit-writing tasks as copying rather than dictation tasks. In the R group only seven of the nineteen children now made a total of thirteen errors, and one of the nineteen children in the NR group made one error. The uncertainty about letter orientation is thus greatly reduced in the copying situation, even though the R group children were poorer in the visual discrimination of shapes.

One can only assume that the level of visual discrimination which the R group children did have was sufficient to enable most of them to 'monitor' their writing of letters and digits in the copying task. However, their discrimination of orientation does not appear to have been sufficiently established to emphasize orientation as a relevant characteristic to remember when the letters and digits were written to dictation. Bryant (1971) found a similar contrast in young children's ability to match shapes when these were simultaneously and successively presented. He postulates that orientational features of a shape are 'coded' in the child's memory according to the setting in which they are presented. It seems possible that the R group children's discrimination of orientation was too poor to make this a feature of the children's memory of the letters and figures. Since the children were poor at reading, this skill was not available to help reduce their uncertainty about letter orientation. In any case, the task only involved writing letters in isolation.

There is some support for the suggestion that children's letter orientation errors are reduced when the letters occur in words. In the Chapman *et al.* study of reversal and transposition errors in 328 children, aged $7\frac{1}{2}$ to $8\frac{1}{2}$, one of the required tasks involved the writing of some of the items from the 'reversible words' subtest of the Daniels and Diack battery. The letters 'b' and 'd' occurred twice in these words, 'd' once as an initial and once as a final letter, 'b' only in the final position. The letter 'b' was found to be reversed more frequently than the letter 'd'. If Marchbanks and Levin (1965) are correct in their finding that children pay most attention to initial letters in reading, then one might suppose that children were more likely to remember the orientation of initial letters. The findings from the Chapman *et al.* study can only be regarded as tentative, but they do suggest that this may be one way in which experience in reading helps to reduce children's uncertainty about letter orientation.

Returning to Chapman and Wedell's (1972) study, it seems likely that the R group's poorer orientation discrimination contributed to their poorer reading, which, in turn, deprived them of some of the constraints on their uncertainty about letter orientation. This kind of explanation would be consistent with the emphasis that has been given here to the interactive effect of sensory organization disabilities and educational performance. It does not, however, explain why these children had difficulty in orientation discrimination in the first place. For this problem one is only left to speculate about the possible implications of the R group's difficulty with the 'crossing of the mid-line task'. Chapman and Wedell feel that this finding needs to be investigated further before its significance can be assessed. It does appear, however, that neither left–right discrimination of body parts nor lateral preference can be regarded as the underlying determinant of orientation errors in handwriting.

This last statement needs to be qualified in respect of left-handed children starting to learn to write. In view of the natural radial movements of the arm, these children often scribble from right to left in 'pretend' writing. This tendency is sometimes carried over when they start to write properly, particularly if the movement pattern in writing is emphasized. It almost seems as though their writing movements are 'programmed' in a sequence, without including an instruction about the direction in which the movements should be made. The child whose writing is shown in Figure 7.2, for example, wrote in mirror fashion if he started on the right side of the page, and properly if he started on the left side of the page. It can be seen that a few letters were not reversed in his mirror writing—for example the 'e's. Clarke (1957) attributes mirror writing to inadequate visual control of the writing movement. An example of this occurs in the writing of the second letter 'e' in the mirror version of the word 'here'. The boy first made a right to left stroke for the middle part of the 'e', and then corrected himself. It should be stressed that the effect of left-handedness on the orientation of

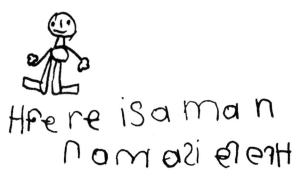

Figure 7.2. Sample of handwriting of a nine-year-old boy

letters in these instances appears to be primarily related to natural movement patterns. If spotted early, these kind of errors can almost always be eradicated without difficulty by clearly showing the child where he should start to write.

Number

It is often stated that children have difficulty in number work because of sensory and motor organization disabilities (Johnson and Myklebust 1967, Cruickshank *et al.* 1966). However, little systematic investigation has been carried out to examine this assumption, and much of the evidence cited takes the form of case examples.

Difficulty with number work has certainly been reported among children with identified sensory and motor organization difficulties. Brenner *et al.* state of the children in their study (1967), 'the school subjects which presented the greatest obstacles to the children with visuo-motor handicap were spelling and arithmetic. In the case of arithmetic, difficulty lay less in connexion with basic principles than with the layout of written work'. It seems that sensory and motor organization difficulties are more likely to handicap a child in performing the mechanics of written computation and in the construction involved in the use of 'concrete' materials, than in the comprehension of arithmetic principles as such. One headmistress cited the case of a child who asked to be allowed to do sums 'in his head', because he became confused if he tried to write the sum down.

Before considering the effects of specific types of disabilities in sensory and motor organization on arithmetic achievement, it is necessary to recall that difficulties in reading and writing will themselves handicap a child's progress in number. Difficulty in reading is likely to have a more extensive effect than difficulty in writing, except, of course, where handwriting difficulty extends to digits. Chapman's study showed that the incidence of wrongly written digits was smaller than that of letters in children aged $7\frac{1}{2}$ to $8\frac{1}{2}$ years, but the incidence of rotated digits was practically as high (see Table 7.2). Many teachers will give the benefit of the doubt to a child who writes the correct answer with rotated figures—at least to the extent of recognizing that his difficulty lies in writing and not in the comprehension of number. However, when a child transposes digits, this distinction becomes more difficult to make.

Modern mathematics teaching has emphasized the importance of the understanding of the concept of quantity. This has led to an increased use of concrete materials with which the child is required to carry out operations involving sensory and motor organization. For example, the child may be given the task of arranging rods in order of size, or constructing models with rods. The child without specific disabilities is able to manipulate these materials with sufficient competence, so that he can begin to build up his concepts of quantity from this experience. The teacher may, however, find that the child with poor sensory and motor organization is having to spend most of his effort on the spatial arrangement of the material—for example, in the construction of a closed figure. The film sequence in Figure 7.3 shows an attempt by a child aged $6\frac{1}{2}$ to copy a square made of rods. The boy was aware of the shape which he was trying to create, but finally had to content himself with making a solid square of blocks. The other sequence illustrated shows that the boy was quite able to make an approximation to an angle.

Piaget has shown the extent to which visual perception determines a child's quantitative judgments, and this insight has led to teaching methods which encourage the child to become independent, for example, of spatial arrangement. The child is led to discover that two sets of six beans are the same quantity, regardless of their spatial arrangement. To the child with difficulties in sensory organization, this switching from one principle of cue selection to another may well present a problem.

Neither of these examples necessarily implies that the child with poor sensory and motor organization should not be taught number in these ways. These activities are likely to constitute valuable training, but it is essential that the teacher should be aware that the child is involved in mastering these more antecedent components of the task. Children with these specific disabilities are likely to depend much more on verbal formulations and labelling when using concrete materials in their acquisition of number concepts.

Sensory and motor organization disability also seem likely to underlie children's difficulty in setting out written sums. The quotation from Brenner given above draws attention to this problem. Some children have considerable difficulty in arranging the tens, units, etc., figures in the appropriate columns and in identifying the correct digit on which to carry out computational operations. Children will subtract the upper digit from the lower digit in a subtraction sum, or confuse the sequence of digits in multiplying.

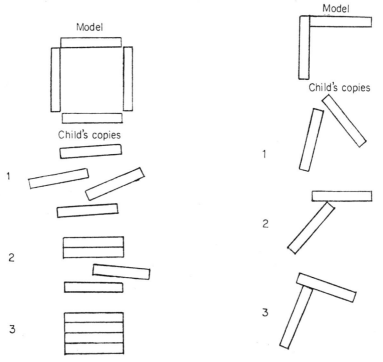

Figure 7.3. Successive stages in a five-year-old child's attempts to copy block models

One factor in children's difficulty with the application of place values is the discrepancy between the sequence in which composite numbers are named and the point of origin of place values. The point of origin of place values is on the right (units, tens, hundreds, etc.) while numbers are named from the highest value downwards (for example, one hundred and twenty-one). Furthermore, in writing out a column of figures, a child has to line the digits up from the right if he is to make the place values correspond vertically. In writing the digits of the number 'one hundred and twenty-one' in a sum, the child with orientation confusion is thus likely to have difficulty in observing the rule that he should line the digits up to a right-hand rather than to a left-hand point of origin, since this conflicts with the left-to-right sequence he has been taught to observe in writing words.

Teachers will be familiar with the child who verbalizes the multiplication sum

$$\begin{array}{r} 17 \\ \times\ 3 \\ \hline \\ \hline \end{array}$$

by saying to himself 'three sevens are twenty-one', writing down the 'two' and carrying the 'one'. This type of difficulty illustrates how the child with an adequate computational knowledge may become involved in error when he writes the results of his computation down. It may also explain the comment quoted earlier of the child who preferred to do sums 'in his head'. However, a child will be able to compensate for direction confusion in this way only to a certain level of computation. Beyond this point, computation will involve holding more numbers 'in his head' than he can manage.

Sensory and motor organization disabilities are likely to constitute a handicap in more advanced mathematics (for example, in geometry). It seems possible that children who may have managed to compensate for their disabilities at lower levels of mathematics may again experience difficulty at those higher levels which involve their deficient skills more specifically. Smith (1964) quotes several studies indicating an association between performance on tests of spatial reasoning and achievement in geometry. Similarly one comes across children who have very particular difficulty in making diagrams in science subjects and in geography.

Auditory perception is likely to be involved in number performance mainly through its relevance for language. Span of auditory attention and auditory memory are clearly of great importance in 'mental' arithmetic. The poor digit memory, noted in many studies of children with learning disabilities, must be a handicap in a wide variety of mathematical classroom tasks. Deficiencies both in visual and in auditory memory are likely to make it more difficult for a child to 'hold' a particular number in 'mental' computation.

There has been some speculation about the association of finger agnosia and poor performance on number tasks in children. Gerstmann (1927) gave his name to a syndrome of symptoms which he claimed to find in some brain-injured adults and which included an impairment in arithmetic calculation and finger agnosia. 'Finger agnosia' refers to a disability in tactile discrimination of the fingers. This is usually assessed by first having the individual close his eyes. One or more of his fingers are then touched and he is asked which and how many of his fingers have been touched. Benton (1961) questioned whether the symptoms occurred together sufficiently frequently to be called a syndrome. Gubbay *et al.* (1965) in their study of twenty-one clumsy children regarded fifteen as showing finger agnosia on Kinsbourne and Warrington's test (1962). Five children were thought to have particular difficulties in arithmetic, but the authors do not state whether these were among those showing finger agnosia. However, even if this had been the case, the finding that ten children with finger agnosia showed no specific arithmetic disability is sufficient to make it unlikely that finger agnosia can be regarded as a cause of failure in arithmetic.

Remediation

Discussion of basic educational attainments in this chapter has repeatedly shown that children have to learn how to apply their sensory and motor organization skills. Children have to learn which sensory cues are relevant to the particular educational task and to monitor their responses with respect to these. Consequently, the absolute level of function in any one aspect of sensory and motor organization has not proved as critical as the extent to which the child has learnt to apply it relevantly.

A considerable number of programmes for the development of sensory and motor organization have been devised. Some of these have already been mentioned in Chapter 6. The initial dearth of evaluation studies is now being made good, but it is becoming increasingly evident that training in general sensory and motor organization has in itself little effect on achievement in specific basic educational attainments. Studies have been carried out in which experimental groups of children have been given remedial activities along the lines of one or other of these programmes, and their progress in reading, for example, has then been compared with the progress made by children receiving ordinary curricular activities, or by children given nonspecific extracurricular 'placebo' activities. The usual finding has then been that, over a period of time, children in both experimental and control groups made some progress in the particular aspect of educational attainment being investigated, but that no significant differences are found between the gains of the experimental and control groups. At the same time, it is frequently found that the experimental group shows a significantly greater increase in performance in those aspects of sensory and motor organization in which they were being specifically trained.

No attempt will here be made to review the results of individual evaluation studies in detail, since this has been done by authors such as Cratty (1970) and Myers and Hammill (1969). Evaluation studies have been criticized by the proponents of the various remedial programmes on several grounds. It has been argued that many of the studies have used children with average attainments in their experimental groups, rather than children who show the kinds of deficits for which the programmes were designed. Another objection that has been made, is that some studies have not carried on the programmes sufficiently long for their effects to become apparent. A third type of criticism has been that those carrying out the programmes with the experimental group children have not been sufficiently motivated or convinced about their effectiveness. Each of these objections can justifiably be applied to one or other of the evaluative studies, but certainly not to all.

One example of an evaluative study that met most of the above criticisms will be considered. O'Bryan and Silverman (1972) report a study in which boys between eight and ten years of age were selected by teachers as showing perceptual handicap. These children were then given an extensive battery of perceptual and motor tests, on the basis of which a group of boys with markedly poor performance was collected. These boys were then randomly allocated to one of three groups. The experimental group was given perceptuo-motor training programmes along the lines devised by Kephart, Frostig and Getman. A 'placebo' group was given a play-activity programme, involving general enrichment activities such as nature hikes, discussions, play-acting, etc. The third group of children constituted the control group and these received normal instruction in their classrooms.

The children in all three groups were retested on the perceptuo-motor and on the achievement tests every six months. At the end of the first six months and after twelve months, no significant differences were found between the groups on any of the measures. After eighteen months, the experimental group was found to have made a significant gain on the perceptuo-motor measures, significantly greater than that of the other two groups. However, these significant differences were not found in educational attainments, although all groups had made educational progress. After two years, the experimental group's perceptuo-motor performance was significantly better than that of the other two groups. The experimental and placebo groups had made significantly greater progress in reading than the control group, but the experimental group's reading was not significantly better than that of the placebo group.

Do findings such as these imply that sensory and motor organization programmes are of no use? It has already been pointed out in Chapter 6 that this is not necessarily an appropriate conclusion. These programmes may develop sensory and motor organization abilities that help the child to achieve general behavioural adequacy. They may do this by virtue of the programme content and by virtue of the systematic and stepwise progression of activities, through which the individual is given definite and limited goals of performance that are within his capacity to achieve. By these means, both the teacher and the child gain confidence, which, in turn, provides motivation for further progress. Silverman and O'Bryan, for example, state that their experimental and placebo group children as well as their teachers, evidenced marked attitudinal improvement early on in their programme. Such findings still raise the question of which aspects of the programme were the effective components, and whether the goals could have been reached more effectively and with less investment of time and staff.

The effectiveness of these programmes in furthering educational achievement is, as has been stated, at least questionable. One or two studies, (for example, Mould 1964) have indicated that some effect on educational progress may be found among younger children. It does seem likely that a programme such as Frostig's, which Mould was investigating, prepares a young child for the attention to visual stimuli that reading instruction demands and for the eye-hand coordination required in beginning to write. However, without training in the application of these skills to educational tasks, little further progress is likely. In fact, this is explicitly stated by Frostig, but these extensions of the activities in her programmes are usually not included in the evaluations of her methods. This is hardly surprising, since it is the 'pre-academic' component of the programme which is open to question. It may be that the subsequent educational progress of children given her programme early is accelerated. Silverman and O'Bryan are continuing to follow up the children in their study, to investigate this possibility. Implications of this kind were found in a study by Radaker (1961) who investigated the effect of visual memory training on subsequent spelling achievement.

A programme ('From Left to Right') devised by Jones attempted, as an integral feature, to provide transfer from training in visual discrimination of orientation to writing letters in their correct position. Jones and Leith (1966) report research findings that this programme was found to be effective in helping ESN children to reduce reversal errors.

The controversy aroused by evaluation studies of sensory and motor organization training programmes revolves to a large extent around the statement of objectives. There is often obscurity about what the programmes are intended to achieve. For example, it may be asked whether a particular programme is intended to provide a better stepwise *preparation* for introducing children to basic educational attainments, or whether it is claimed that the programme will improve the attainment levels of children who have already started and have failed. Clearly claims about transfer are implicit in the latter but not the former objective. It would seem profitable for those who are carrying out evaluation studies to get together with the authors of the programmes to be studied. It is often difficult for an educator to evaluate his own particular methods and such a cooperative approach might encourage authors to state their objectives more clearly, so that evaluators can choose their criteria appropriately. As a result, the 'baby' of effective special educational methods might not be thrown out with the 'bathwater' of unsubstantiated claims.

CHAPTER 8

Conclusion

This book has focused on one particular aspect of the 'equipment' with which the child interacts with his environment. Sensory and motor organization functions have been distinguished, on the one hand from receptor and effector functions, and on the other from the conceptual structure which the child establishes through the mediation of his sensory organization. It will have become evident that drawing the limits imposed by such a specific focus was not always an easy matter, and often seemed somewhat arbitrary. At the same time, the specific study of these functions led to a consideration of findings from both psychological and educational research, and indicated the extent to which these two areas of work supplemented each other.

It has been interesting to note that the very attempt to limit consideration to this one specific group of functions has highlighted the interdependence of sensory and motor organization and other functions. The handicaps resulting from deficiencies in sensory and motor organization have been identified, but it has also become evident that normal functional levels in other areas enable the child to compensate for these deficiencies to a large extent. Within the child, the compensatory roles of language and conceptual development have been stressed. In the child's environment, the compensatory potential both of parental handling and of good teaching have emerged.

All these considerations have shown that it is very difficult to predict the level of behavioural and educational adequacy which a child with deficient sensory and motor organization may achieve. People working in this field are familiar with children who perform on educational tasks at a standard which the level of their performance on tests of sensory and motor organization would seem to make impossible. So it seems that while one may be justified in ascribing behavioural or educational inadequacy in a child to deficiencies in sensory and motor organization, one can only *predict* poor achievement in a child on the basis of very severe deficiency in these functions. From a theoretical point of view, such a 'non-reciprocal' causal relationship may seem unsatisfactory. From a practical point of view, it is extremely fortunate, because it emphasizes the compensatory potential available to a child. If prediction on the basis of *functional* assessment proves as difficult as this, it is not surprising that prediction on the basis of medical diagnoses of organic defects is likely to be even more uncertain.

The lack of a basis for prediction need not deter one, however, from studying concomitance. Much of the research quoted has shown the concomitance of sensory and motor organization disabilities with organic conditions on the one hand, and with behavioural and educational inadequacy on the other. Such parallels have thrown up useful theoretical models, which, in turn, have indicated ways in which investigations can be sharpened by greater specificity. Studies of children with learning disabilities have, however, often seduced special educators into making causal inferences from findings of a regular association of two conditions. This fall from scientific grace is, of course, very prevalent, but it has presented a major stumbling block in the growth of understanding of learning disabilities. Symptoms such as difficulty in left–right discrimination of body parts, for example, have been found in children showing learning disabilities, and have been elevated to the status of causes rather than concomitants. This, in turn, has led some special educators to formulate hypothetical constructs such as 'body image', which are then converted into educational goals in their own right, without any firm evidence that their achievement will be relevant to the child's needs.

As a general point one might say that workers in the field of sensory and motor organization disabilities should distinguish their role as special educators or clinicians, from their role as researchers. As special educators or clinicians concerned with an individual child's educational or behavioural failure, they can judge the handicapping effect of sensory or motor organization disabilities only on the basis of an analysis of the child's current performance, or on a retrospective analysis of his development. On the other hand, as researchers, they should be very much concerned with investigating the predictive implications of sensory and motor organization deficits for later behavioural or educational handicap.

This point underlies the current issue among educators concerning the choice of educational objectives. There are those who maintain that educational goals should be defined in terms of the specific tasks on which a child is found to fail. If the child cannot read, teach him to read; if he is hyperactive, teach him to be still in the situations where his activity presents a problem. Those opposing this view would argue that, in a broad category of children, deficiencies in sensory and motor organization can be seen as the main cause of their failure. Furthermore, one should therefore, direct remediation at these functions because they subserve a wide range of the child's performance, and because improvement in them will generalize correspondingly. Some would go further and argue that training in sensory and motor organization functions will produce neuro-physiological changes and, by enhancing organic efficiency, will improve the child's functioning over a wider front.

The basis of this argument is that intervention concentrated on deficiencies in key functions produces greater generality of improvement than attempts to remediate each particular failure that the child shows.

Throughout this book, the point has been made that it is difficult to make general statements about the relevance of sensory and motor organization functions to a particular child's performance on a particular task. The claim that sensory and motor organization deficiencies can be *assumed* to underlie certain types of impaired performance would thus be questioned. This still leaves the claim about generalization of the effects of sensory and motor organization training. As far as educational attainments are concerned, the research findings on the effect of sensory and motor organization programmes have not provided support for the claim of generalized positive effect. Furthermore, research evidence strongly indicates that the child needs to learn how to apply his sensory and motor organization skills to the specific educational task. Help for failure in basic educational attainments would therefore seem to be best directed at those attainments themselves. It is worth pursuing the implications of this statement, because they in fact lead one back to the need for training in sensory and motor organization skills. While the basic premises of the two special educational orientations that have been compared here are very different, it is interesting to note that the practical outcomes of their application are not so dissimilar.

If one looks at the child failing in basic educational attainments, as was done in Chapter 7, and analyses what he can and cannot do, one may well trace the child's problems back to deficiencies in the sensory or motor organization components of the educational task and find oneself teaching visual or auditory discrimination, or motor organization skills in a form that is little different from that proposed in some of the sensory and motor organization programmes that have been discussed. The main difference will be that the objectives of these activities will be more limited and that training for transfer to the next level of the educational skill will be emphasized. However, in some programmes such training for transfer is in fact specifically recommended.

It is less easy to extend the argument to the remediation of failure in behavioural adequacy. It has already been pointed out that little work has been done on the definition of criteria for behavioural adequacy. It is difficult to say what are the particular tasks in which one expects proficiency at given ages and, furthermore, what level of proficiency one expects. In the absence of specific objectives, one might well argue in favour of programmes directed at the improvement of sensory and motor organization in general. Furthermore, if a list of specific objectives was drawn up, it would be so long that it might be thought impracticable to devise task-oriented programmes for each one. This is clearly an area where much more research is required. As was stressed in Chapter 6, sensory and motor organization programmes should be assessed for their effect on aspects of children's behavioural adequacy. Evaluation studies along these lines would seem to be of prime importance. For example, a project is currently being undertaken to examine the effectiveness of a programme based on Kephart's methods, for seven- to ten-year-old 'clumsy' children. Functional criteria have been set up for evaluating the effectiveness with which a child is able to move around without bumping into objects. This seemed an appropriate set of criteria to apply to a programme which was aimed at the improvement of 'body image'. For example, children are required to step over and under horizontal bars without touching them, to reach between objects without bumping into them, and to perform similar tasks intended to reveal their knowledge of the extension in space of their body parts. The children's performance is being analysed from film records. One group of clumsy children is being given activities along Kephart's lines, and another group is being given the normal physical education curriculum. The children are all in a residential school, and consequently it is possible to keep the environment of the two groups the same.

The discussion, in Chapters 3 and 6, of research findings indicating the possible importance of very early stages in the development of sensory organization suggests that functional criteria should be set up already for the infant. For example, if habituation rate is confirmed as a relevant aspect of the child's functioning at the infant stage, criteria of adequacy should be established, so that gross deficiencies could be recognized and, hopefully, acted upon. It should be stressed that the grounds for such intervention would be that habituation constituted an aspect of the child's *expected* performance. In view of the arguments put forward above, one would not wish to direct 'remediation' at habituation rate in the form of a hypothetical construct.

Needless to say, the present state of knowledge about the relevance of these early stages of sensory organization is a long way from the point at which it could support such practical implications. Deviations from normal functioning would probably have to be considerable to be of predictive significance. However, there are few other behavioural variables available for assessment in these early months.

The development of behaviour observation techniques is likely to provide us with one means of specifying criteria of behavioural adequacy in the pre-school child. Observation of children's behaviour in an experimental setting such as that used by the Hutts (mentioned in Chapter 6) is likely to yield not only means of defining behavioural adequacy, but also useful hypotheses about the processes underlying behaviour.

Much more information is needed about the development of the child's motor organization skills in everyday tasks. In the meantime, however, more significance should be ascribed to individual variations in the two- to five-year-old's performance on the whole range of self-help skills from dressing to steering a tricycle. It seems likely that components of existing sensory and motor organization programmes might well provide much of the training that would be relevant for these tasks.

One further point needs to be made about the application of sensory and motor organization programmes. There seems to be an inherent implication that educational efforts should be directed at children's weaknesses. The issue of whether one should teach to a child's strengths or weaknesses is frequently raised by teachers. From the emphasis given in this book to the interaction between a child's abilities and disabilities, it should now be clear that such an issue is likely to be false. Education should be directed at both a child's strengths and his weaknesses. For example, the child whose written work is terrible should not be made to express himself solely in a written form. He should be given opportunity to express himself orally, and even to record his compositions on a tape recorder, if this is feasible. At the same time he should be given specific handwriting instruction. It is likely that oral practice in organizing his ideas will reduce his uncertainty about what he wants to say, and so at least reduce some of the messiness in his written work resulting from 'crossing out'. The educator will have to gauge the stage at which efforts to improve handwriting reach a point of diminishing return and, if necessary, modify his goals.

In this final section of the chapter, implications for planning identification and intervention procedures for children with sensory and motor organization disabilities will be discussed. The points which will be made will frequently apply to children with a wider range of special educational needs.

The need for early identification has already been stressed, and so has the fact that identification needs to be based on demonstrated rather than inferred deficiency. Before the child goes to school, the only people in a position to evaluate his behaviour are his parents, the family doctor and, in England, the Health Visitor. Even considering the fact that there is very little relevant normative information available on the basis of which deficient functioning could be assessed, one has to admit that the chances for early identification are not very good. Parents certainly tend not to be good judges of their children's progress, being frequently either too demanding or too undemanding. There is clearly scope here for better training in parenthood in secondary schools. One would strongly support the recommendations that have recently been made, for making child development and other aspects of knowledge useful for parents an extensively treated topic in the upper years of secondary school.

It has to be admitted that the situation also occurs, where a parent in fact correctly assesses his child as underfunctioning, but is told when he takes him to the doctor, that the child 'will grow out of it'. The need for improved training in child development for doctors is now fortunately recognized. However, even so, the doctor can only evaluate the child who is brought to him.

This is where the Health Visitor plays such an important part in the United Kingdom. In view of her responsibility to 'keep an eye' on the development of all the children in a particular district, she is in a unique position to identify those children who are likely to be in need of help. When I have spoken in the United States and Canada about the work of Health Visitors in England, anxieties about *Nineteen Eighty-Four* type 'Big Brother' supervision have been raised. In fact this problem does not arise, since the Health Visitor functions in an advisory capacity. Here, then, is someone who can not only evaluate the functional level of the child, but also the environmental resources available to help him.

Identification of deficiency need not necessarily be followed immediately by intervention. In the short term, and before the parents may have expressed concern, the only requisite action may be further observation. If development continues to be handicapped, or if the parents begin to feel there is a problem, suggestions about minor modifications, for instance in handling, may be made. From clinical experience one knows of instances where parents have been enabled to help a child over moderate levels of hyperactivity by minor modifications in handling such as more explicit verbal controls or daily routines. It is well known that minor early intervention of this kind can help the hyperactive child, for example, to develop his own behavioural controls. Parents themselves usually long to be able to do something to help their children. All too often it is assumed that they are incapable of providing appropriate help and are left to manage their handicapped children with frustrated bewilderment. On the other hand, the increased confidence which parents gain from helping their children even in limited and rather obvious ways, which may not have occurred to them, may change a family atmosphere from desperation to constructive hope.

Where parents are unable to provide such added support to a child, where circumstances do not permit it, or when the problem fails to respond to such modifications, further intervention such as nursery school attendance can then be brought into action.

The above line of action for identification and intervention is thus based not only on evaluation of the child, but also on evaluation of the environmental support available to him. Remedial action from an outside agency is initiated only when the interaction between the child and his environment does not result in a reduction of the child's handicap.

It must be stressed that the above emphasis on the assessment both of normal development and of progress resulting from extra help, puts a great deal of weight on a knowledge of normal development and its 'normal' variations. In a systematized form such knowledge is as yet only rudimentary, but it has to be acknowledged that the quality of intuitive judgment on the part of the professionals concerned often compensates for this lack. A more serious deficiency is, of course, lack of personnel, and of facilities for referral.

Most of the comments made about identification and intervention for the pre-school child, apply also to the handicapped school-age child. School, of course, imposes a whole range of more specific expectations about behavioural and educational adequacy in the child, and the early school years usually provide a peak in referral rates for a variety of problems. Nonetheless, in many ways, expectations are still not sufficiently explicitly formulated to help the teacher recognize a child's failure at an early stage. Even where a teacher notices that a child is failing, two considerations often inhibit him in acting on his assessment. First, the teacher may be reluctant to formulate his fears about a child sufficiently to ask for outside help, because he fears that the child will be irrevocably 'labelled' as deficient or even removed to some unknown form of special provision. Second, the teacher may in fact recognize a child's failure to function up to expectation but ascribe this to 'slow development' or 'deprived background' with the implication that these factors make the child's progress unmodifiable.

Teachers, especially those dealing with children in their early school years, need to be helped to a much greater knowledge of child development and to more specific expectations of behavioural and educational competency. This knowledge should certainly be geared to the local characteristics of the children they are teaching, but should be sufficiently specific to enable them to assess minor inadequacies of development. Just as with the pre-school child, such identification of deficiency should be followed by an initial period of further observation and by minor intervention if necessary. This may be carried out with or without outside professional advice, according to the teacher's own competence. However, outside *intervention* would only be brought in when these initial measures did not lead to sufficient progress. Such an approach to early intervention for children with specific deficiencies is again limited at present by the dearth of our knowledge. Unless expectations about developmental progress are specific, informal assessment and intervention cannot be carried on a sufficiently short-term basis to be effective.

This discussion of specific deficiencies in the early school years has again brought out that the child's need for help is evaluated on the basis of the interaction between the child's functional deficiencies and assets, and the compensatory potential of his school—and home—environment. For example, it is very evident, from the findings of the Educational Priority

Area research projects, that children in different schools but from the same deprivational background may achieve widely divergent rates of progress.

The plea made in Chapter 1, that we should concern ourselves not so much with the classifications of handicapped children, but more with an analysis of the deficits they show, thus needs to be extended. As Adelman (1971) has pointed out we need not only to assess the specific functional assets and deficits of the individual child, but also to assess the compensatory potential of the particular environment in which the child's behavioural or educational inadequacy is shown.

It is hoped that the discussion of sensory and motor organization in this book has made one part of the child's side of this equation a little clearer.

References

Abercrombie, M. L. J. *et al.* (1964), Visual, perceptual and visuo motor impairment in physically handicapped children, *Perceptual and Motor Skills*, **18**, 561–625

Abercrombie, M. L. J., and Tyson, M. C. (1966), Body image and draw-a-man test in cerebral palsy, *Developmental Medicine and Child Neurology*, **8**, 9–15

Adams, P. A. (1969), Handwriting disabilities in educationally handicapped children; a sibling study. Paper read at the Society for Research in Child Development, Santa Monica

Adelman, H. S. (1970, 1971), Learning problems: an interactional view of causality; Part I and Part II, *Academic Therapy*, **6**, (2), 117–24 and **6**, (3), 287–92

Albitreccia, S. I. (1958), Recognition and treatment of disturbance of body image, *Celebral Palsy Bulletin*, **4**, 12–17

Allen, R. M., Dickman I., and Haupt, T, (1966), A pilot study of the immediate effectiveness of the Frostig-Horne training program with educable retardates, *Exceptional Children*, **31**, 41

Anderson, N. S., and Leonard, J. A. (1958), The recognition, naming and reconstruction of visual figures as a function of contour redundancy, *Journal of Experimental Psychology*, **56**, 262–70

Annett, M., Lee, D., and Ounsted, C. D. (1961), Intellectual disabilities in relation to lateralised features in the E.E.G., *Little Club Clinics in Developmental Medicine*, **4**, 86–112

Apgar, V., and James, L. S. (1962), Further observations on the newborn scoring system, *American Journal of the Diseases of Children*, **104**, 419–28

Ayres, A. J. (1965), Patterns of perceptual-motor dysfunction in children: a factor analytic study, *Perceptual and Motor Skills*, **20**, 335–68

Ayres, A. J. (1966), Interrelations among perceptual-motor abilities in a group of normal children, *American Journal of Occupational Therapy*, **20**, 288–92

Ayres, A. J. (1968), Effect of sensorimotor activity on perception and learning in neurologically handicapped children. Unpublished report, University of Southern California

Bannatyne, A. D., and Wichiarajote, P. (1969), Relationships between written spelling, motor functioning and sequencing skills, *Journal of Learning Disabilities*, **2**, 4–16

Barrett, M. L., and Jones, M. H. (1967), The 'Sensory Story'; a multisensory training procedure for toddlers, *Developmental Medicine and Child Neurology*, **9**, 448–56

Barrett, T. C. (1965), The relationship between measures of pre-reading visual discrimination and first grade reading achievement, *Reading Research Quarterly*, **1**, (1), 51–76

Barry, H. (1961), *The Young Aphasic Child*, Graham Bell Association

Bateman, B. (1967), The efficacy of an auditory and visual method of first-grade reading instruction with auditory and visual learners, *Curriculum Bulletin*, **23**, (278), 6–14

Belmont, L., and Birch, H. G. (1966), The intellectual profile of retarded readers, *Perceptual and Motor Skills*, **22**, 787–816

Bensberg, G. J. (1952), The relation of academic achievement of mental defectives to mental age, sex, institutionalisation and etiology, *American Journal of Mental Deficiency*, **58**, 327–30

Benton, A. L. (1959), *Right-Left Discrimination and Finger Localisation*, P. B. Hoeber

Benton, A. L. (1961), The fiction of the 'Gerstmann Syndrome', *Journal of Neurology, Neurosurgery and Psychiatry*, **24**, 176–81

Bereiter, C., and Engelmann, S. (1966), *Teaching Disadvantaged Children in the Pre-School*, Prentice Hall.

Berger, Barbara (1969), A longitudinal investigation of Montessori and traditional pre-kindergarten training with inner city children: a comparative assessment of learning outcomes, *Center for Urban Education*

Berko, M. J. (1954), Some factors in the perceptual deviations of cerebral palsied children, *Cerebral Palsy Review*, **15**, (3–4), 14

Birch, H. G. (ed.) (1964), *Brain damage in children*, Williams and Wilkins Co.

Birch, H. G., and Belmont, L. (1965), Auditory-visual integration, intelligence and reading ability in school children, *Perceptual and Motor Skills*, **20**, 295–305

Birch, H. G., and Lefford, A. (1967), Visual differentiation, intersensory integration and voluntary motor control, *Child Development Monographs*, **32**, No. 2

Bond, G. L., and Tinker, M. A. (1967), *Reading Difficulties: Their Diagnosis and Correction* (2nd edn.), Appleton-Century-Crofts

Bortner, M., and Birch, H. G. (1962), Perceptual and perceptual-motor dissociation in cerebral palsied children, *Journal of Nervous and Mental Diseases*, **134**, 103–8

Bower, T. G. R. (1966), Slant perception and shape constancy in infants, *Science*, **151**, 832–4

Boyd, L., and Randle, K. (1970), Factor analysis of the Frostig developmental test of visual perception, *Journal of Learning Disabilities*, **3**, 253–5

Brenner, M. W., and Gillman, S. (1966), Visuomotor ability in school children —a survey, *Developmental Medicine and Child Neurology*, **8**, 686–703

Brenner, M. W., Gillman, S., Zangwill, O. L. and Farrell, M. (1967), Visuomotor disability in school children, *British Medical Journal*, **4**, 259–62

Brimer, M. A., and Dunn, L. M. (1963), *Manual for the English Picture Vocabulary Tests*, National Foundation for Educational Research

Brown, R. I. (1966), The effects of varied environmental stimulation on the performance of subnormal children, *Journal of Child Psychology and Psychiatry*, **7**, 251–61

Bruner, J. S. (1970), The growth and structure of skill, in Connolly, K. (ed.), *Mechanisms of Motor Skill Development*, Academic Press

Bryant, P. E. (1971) Cognitive development, *British Medical Bulletin*, **27**, (3), 200–5

Chall, J. S. (1967), *Learning to Read: The Great Debate*, McGraw-Hill

Chapman, J., Lewis, A., and Wedell, K. (1970), A note reversals in the writing of eight-year-old children, *Remedial Education*, **5**, 91–4

Chapman, J., and Wedell, K. (1972), Perceptuo-motor abilities and reversal errors in children's handwriting, *Journal of Learning Disabilities*, **5**, 321–5

Clarke, M. M. (1957), *Left Handedness*, Oxford University Press

Cobrinik, L. (1959), Performance of brain-injured children on hidden-figure tasks, *American Journal of Psychology*, **72**, 566–71

Cohen, J. (1959), The factorial structure of the WISC at ages 7–6, 10–6 and 13–6, *Journal of Consulting Psychology*, **23**, 285–99

Cohen, L. B., Gelber, E. R., and Lazar, M. A. (1971), Infant habituation and generalization to repeated visual stimulation, *Journal of Experimental Child Psychology*, **11**, 379–89

Connolly, K. (1968), The implications of operant conditioning to the measurement and development of motor skill in children, *Developmental Medicine and Child Neurology*, **10**, 697–705

Connolly, K. (1970), Skill development: problems and plans, in Connolly, K. (ed.), *Mechanisms of Motor Skill Development*, Academic Press

Corah, N. L., and Powell, B. J. (1963), A factor analytic study of the Frostig test of visual perception, *Perceptual and Motor Skills*, **16**, 59–63

Cratty, B. J. (1970), *Perceptual and Motor Development in Infants and Children*, Collier-Macmillan

Cronbach, L. J. (1960), *Essentials of Psychological Testing* (2nd edn.), Harper and Row

Cruickshank, W. M. *et al.* (1961), *A teaching method for brain-injured and hyperactive children*, (Syracuse University Special Education and Rehabilitation Monograph Series 6), Syracuse University Press

Cruickshank, W. M. *et al.* (1965), *Perception and Cerebral Palsy* (revised edn.), Syracuse University Press

Cruickshank, W. M. (ed.), 1966, *The teacher of brain-injured children*, (Syracuse University Special Education and Rehabilitation Monograph Series No. 7)

Daniels, J. C., and Diack, H. (1970), *The Standard Reading Tests*, Chatto and Windus

Day, J., and Wedell, K. (1972), Visual and auditory memory in spelling: an exploratory study, *British Journal of Educational Psychology*, **42**, 33–9

Dayton, G. O. *et al.* (1964), Developmental study of coordinated eye movements in the human infant, *Archives of Ophthalmology*, **71**, 865–70

De Hirsch, K., Jansky, J. J., and Langford, W. S. (1966), *Predicting Reading Failure*, Harper and Row

Delacato, C. H. (1963), *The Diagnosis and Treatment of Speech and Reading Problems*, Chas. C. Thomas

Denhoff, E. (1966), Cerebral palsy: medical aspects, in Cruickshank, W. M. (ed.), *Cerebral Palsy* (2nd edn.), Syracuse University Press

De Occampo, G. (1954), Psychosomatic aspects of ophthalmology, *Journal of the Philippine Medical Association*, **30**, (2), 65–73

Diack, H. (1960), *Reading and the Psychology of Perception*, Peter Skinner

Durkin, D. (1969), A two year language arts program for pre-first grade children, (First year report). Paper given at the annual conference of the American Educational Research Association

Dykstra, R. (1966), Auditory discrimination abilities and beginning reading achievement, *Reading Research Quarterly*, **1**, 5–34

Eames, T. H. (1964), The effect of anisometropia on reading achievement, *American Journal of Optometry and Archives of the American Academy of Optometry*, **41**, 700–2

Edgar, C. L., Ball, T. S., McIntyre, R. B., and Shotwell, A. M. (1969), Effects of sensory-motor training on adaptive behavior, *American Journal of Mental Deficiency*, **73**, 713–20

Eisenberg, L. (1966), The management of the hyperkinetic child, *Developmental Medicine and Child Neurology*, **8**, 593–8

Espenschade, A. S., and Eckert, H. M. (1967), *Motor Development*, C. E. Merrill

Fantz, R. L. (1963), Pattern vision in newborn infants, *Science*, **140**, 296–7

Fellows, B. J. (1968), *Discrimination Process and Development*, Pergamon

Fernald, G. M. (1943), *Remedial Techniques in Basic School Subjects*, McGraw-Hill

Frostig, M. (1963), Visual perception in the brain-injured child, *American Journal of Orthopsychiatry*, **33**, 665–71

Frostig, M. (1966), *Manual for the Marianne Frostig Developmental Test of Visual Perception*, Consulting Psychologists Press

Frostig, M., and Horne, D. (1964), *Frostig Program for the Development of Visual Perception—Teachers' Guide,* Follett Publishing Co.

Frostig, M., and Maslow, P. (1970), *Movement Education: Theory and Practice*, Follett Educational Corporation

Furth, H. (1966), *Thinking Without Language*, Collier-Macmillan

Gates, A. I. (1922), The psychology of reading and spelling, *Teachers' College Contributions in Education*, (1922), No. 129

Gates, A. I. (1926), A study of the role of visual perception, intelligence and certain associative processes in reading and spelling, *Journal of Educational Psychology*, **17**, 433

Gerstmann, J. (1927), Fingeragnosie und isolierte agraphie. Ein neuer syndrom, *Zeitschrift der gesamten Neurologie und Psychiatrie*, **108**, 152–77

Gesell, A., and Ilg, F. I. (1949), *Child Development*, Harper Bros.

Ghent, L. (1960), Recognition by children of realistic figures in various orientations, *Canadian Journal of Psychology*, **14** (4), 249–56

Gibson, E. J. (1965), Learning to read, *Science*, **148**, 1066–72

Gibson, E. J. (1969), *Principles of Perceptual Learning and Development*, Appleton-Century-Crofts

Gibson, E. J., Gibson, J. J., Pick, A. D., and Osser, H. A. (1962), Developmental study of the discrimination of letter-like forms, *Journal of Comparative and Physiological Psychology*, **55**, 897–906

Gibson, E. J., Osser, H., and Pick, A. D. (1963), A study in the development of grapheme-phoneme correspondence, *Journal of Verbal Learning and Verbal Behaviour*, **2**, 142–6

Gibson, E. J., and Walk, R. D. (1960), The 'visual cliff', *Scientific American*, **202**, 64–71

Goins, J. T. (1958), Visual perceptual abilities and early reading progress, *Supplementary Educational Monographs*, No. 87

Goldfarb, W. (1964), An investigation of childhood schizophrenia, *Archives of General Psychiatry*, **2**, 620–34

Goodenough, F. L. (1926), *Measurement of Intelligence by Drawing*, Harcourt, Brace and World

Goodman, K. S. (ed.) (1968), *The Psycholinguistic Nature of the Reading Process*, Wayne State University Press

Griffiths, R. (1970), *Griffiths Mental Developmental Scales*, Child Development Research Centre

Gubbay, S. S., Ellis, E., Walton, J. N., and Court, S. D. M. (1965), Clumsy children, a study of apraxic and agnosic defects in 21 children. *Brain*, **88**, 295–312

Haith, M. M. (1966), Response of the human newborn to movement, *Journal of Experimental Child Psychology*, **3**, 235–43

Hallahan, D. P. (1970), Cognitive styles—preschool implications for the disadvantaged, *Journal of Learning Disabilities*, **3**, 4–11

Halpin, V. G., and Patterson, R. (1958), Basic issues concerning the education of children with cerebral defects, *American Journal of Mental Deficiency*, **63**, 31–7

Harris, D. B. (1963), *Children's Drawings as Measures of Intellectual Maturity*, Harcourt, Brace and World

Haskell, S., and Hughes, V. A. (1965), Some observations on the performance of squinters and non-squinters on the Wechsler intelligence scale for children, *Perceptual and Motor Skills*, **21**, 107–12

Hecaen, H., and Ajuriaguerra, J. (1964), *Left-handedness*, Grune and Stratton

Hermelin, B., and O'Connor, N. (1970), *Psychological Experiments with Autistic Children*, Pergamon

Hewett, F. M. (1968), *The Emotionally Disturbed Child in the Classroom*, Allyn and Bacon

Hill, J. P. (ed.) (1967), *Minnesota Symposia on Child Psychology I*, University of Minnesota Press

Hill, J. P. (ed.) (1968), *Minnesota Symposia on Child Psychology II*, University of Minnesota Press

Hill, S., McCullum, A., and Sceau, A. (1967), Relation of training in motor activity to development of right-left directionality in mentally retarded children, *Perceptual and Motor Skills*, **24**, 363–6

Hiskey, M. S. (1966), *Hiskey-Nebraska Test of Learning Aptitude-Manual*, Union College Press

Holt, K. S., and Reynell, J. K. (1967), *Assessment of Cerebral Palsy*, Lloyd-Luke

Horn, J., and Quarmby, J. (1970), The problem of older non-readers, *Special Education*, **59**, (3), 23–5

Howard, I. P., and Templeton, W. B. (1966), *Human Spatial Orientation*, Wiley

Hutt, S. J., and Hutt, C. (1964), Hyperactivity in a group of epileptic (and some non-epileptic) brain damaged children, *Epilepsia*, **5**, 334–51

Hutt, S. J., and Hutt, C. (1970), *Behaviour Studies in Psychiatry*, Pergamon

Jeffrey, W. E. (1958), Variables in early discrimination learning: I. motor responses in the training of a left-right discrimination, *Child Development*, **29**, 269–75

Jeffrey, W. E. (1968), The orienting reflex and attention in cognitive development, *Psychological Review*, **75**, 323–34

Jeffrey, W. E. (1971), Habituation in the human infant, in Reese, H. W. (ed.), *Advances in Child Development and Behaviour Volume 6*, Academic Press

Johnson, D. J., and Myklebust, H. (1967), *Learning Disabilities*, Grune and Stratton

Jones, C. H., and Leith, G. O. M. (1966), Programming an aspect of reading readiness, *Remedial Education*, **1**, 5–8

Kagan, J. (1969), On the meaning of behaviour: illustrations from the infant, *Child Development*, **40**, 1121–34

Kagan, J., Henker, B. A., Hentov, A., Levine, J., and Levis, M. (1966), Infants' differential reactions to familiar and distorted faces, *Child Development*, **37**, 519–32

Keogh, B. K. (1971), A compensatory model for psychoeducational evaluation of children with learning disorders, *Journal of Learning Disabilities*, **4**, 544–8

Keogh, B. K., and Keogh, J. F. (1967), Pattern copying and pattern walking performance of normal and educationally subnormal boys, *American Journal of Mental Deficiency*, **71**, 1009–13

Keogh, B. K., and Smith, C. E. (1961), Group techniques and proposed scoring system for the Bender-gestalt test with children, *Journal of Clinical Psychology*, **17**, 172–5

Keogh, B. K., and Smith, C. E. (1967), Visuo-motor ability for school prediction: a seven year study, *Perceptual and Motor Skills*, **25**, 101–10

Keogh, J. F. (1965), *Motor Performance of Elementary School Children*, Dept. of Physical Education, University of California at Los Angeles

Keogh, J. F. (1968), A rhythmical hopping task as an assessment of motor deficiency. Paper read at Second International Congress of Sport Psychology Washington DC.

Kephart, N. C. (1960), *The Slow Learner in the Classroom*, C. E. Merrill

Kerschner, J. R. (1968), Doman Delacato's theory of neurological organization applied with retarded children, *Exceptional Children*, **34**, 441–52

Kidd, A. H., and Rivoire, J. L. (1966), *Perceptual Development in Children*, University of London Press

Kinsbourne, M., and Warrington, E. K. (1962), A study of finger agnosia, *Brain*, **85**, 47–67

Kirk, S. A. (1966), *Diagnosis and Remediation of Psycholinguistic Disabilities*, Institute for Research on Exceptional Children, University of Illinois

Kirk, S. A., McCarthy, J. J., and Kirk, W. D. (1968), *Illinois Test of Psycholinguistic Abilities* (Revised edn.), University of Illinois

Klaus, R. A., and Gray, S. W. (1968), The early training project for disadvantaged children; a report after five years, *Monographs of the Society for Research in Child Development*, **33**, (4)

Koppitz, E. (1964), *The Bender Gestalt Test for Young Children*, Grune Stratton

Larr, A. L. (1956), Perceptual and conceptual abilities of residential school deaf children, *Exceptional Children*, **23**, 63–6

Lewis, H. R., and Lewis, H. P. (1964), Which manuscript letters are hard for first graders? *Elementary English*, **41**, 855–8

Lewis, M. (1970), Individual differences in the measurement of early cognitive growth, *Research Bulletin; Educational Testing Service*, No. 9

Lewis, M., Bartels, B., Campbell, H., and Goldberg, S. (1967), Individual differences in attention: the relation between infants' condition at birth and attention distribution within the first year, *American Journal of Diseases of Children*, **113**, 461–5

Lewis, M., and Goldberg, S. (1969), Perceptual-cognitive development in infancy, *Merrill-Palmer Quarterly*, **15**, 81–100

Lewis, M., Goldberg, S., and Campbell, H. (1969), A developmental study of information processing with the first three years of life: response decrement to a redundant signal, *Monographs of the Society for Research in Child Development*, **34**, No. 9

Leydorf, M. (1971), Physical-motor factors, in Keogh, B. (ed.), Early identification of children with potential learning problems, *Journal of Special Education*, **4**, 313–19

Lines, G. W. R., and Widlake, P. (1971), Literacy in primary schools, in *Report on the Birmingham Educational Priority Area Action Research Project*

Livingston, A. A. (1961), A study of spelling errors, in Scottish Council for Research in Education, *Studies in spelling*, University of London Press

Lovell, K. (1959), A follow-up study of some aspects of the work of Piaget and Inhelder on the child's conception of space, *British Journal of Educational Psychology*, **29**, 104–17

Lowenfeld, M. (1929), *Mosaic Test*, Badger Test Co. Ltd.

Luria, A. R. (1961), *The Role of Speech in the Regulation of Normal and Abnormal Behaviour*, Pergamon

Luria, A. R. (1963), *The Mentally Retarded Child*, Pergamon

Maccoby, E. E. (1967), Selective auditory attention in children, in Lipsitt, L. P. and Spiker, C. C. (eds.), *Advances in Child Development and Behaviour III*, Academic Press

McCall, R. B., and Kagan, J. (1970), Individual differences in the infant's distribution of attention to stimulus discrepancy, *Developmental Psychology*, **2**, 90–8

McDill, E. L., McDill, M. S., and Sprehe, J. T. (1969), *Strategies for Success In Compensatory Education: An Appraisal of Evaluation Research*, Johns Hopkins Press

McFie, J. (1961a), Intellectual impairment in children with localised post infantile cerebral lesions, *Journal of Neurology, Neurosurgery and Psychiatry*, **24**, 361–5

McFie, J. (1961b), The effects of hemispherectomy on intellectual functioning in cases of hemiplegia, *Journal of Neurology, Neurosurgery and Psychiatry*, **24**, 240–9

Mangan, K. R. (1963), The deaf, in Kirk, S. A. and Blumer, W. B., *Behavioural Research on Exceptional Children*, Council for Exceptional Children

Marchbanks, G., and Levin, H. (1965), Cues by which children recognize words, *Journal of Educational Psychology*, **56**, 57–61

Maslow, P. *et al.* (1964), The Marianne–Frostig Developmental Test of Visual Perception 1963 standardization, *Perceptual and Motor Skills*, **19**, 463–99

Maxwell, A. E. (1959), A factor analysis of the WISC, *British Journal of Educational Psychology*, **29**, 237–41

Miller, N. E., Galanter, E., and Pribram, K. H. (1960), *Plans and the Structure of Behaviour*, Holt

Morris, J. (1966), *Standards and Progress in Reading*, National Foundation for Educational Research

Morris, P. R., and Whiting, H. T. A. (1971), *Motor Impairment and Compensatory Education*, Bell

Mould, R. (1964), An evaluation of the effectiveness of a special program for retarded readers manifesting disturbed visual perception. Unpublished Ph.D. thesis: Washington State University

Munn, N. L. (1965), *The Evolution and Growth of Human Behaviour*, (2nd edn.), Harrap

Murphy, K. P. (1962), *Ascertainment of deafness in children*, Panorama 3 December

Murphy, M., and McHugh, M. (1971), Comparative evaluation of three methods for the remedial teaching of spelling to mildly handicapped children with perceptual handicaps, *Bulletin of the British Psychological Society*, **24**, 341

Myers, P. I., and Hammill, D. D. (1969), *Methods for Learning Disorders*, Wiley

Myklebust, H. R. (1954), *Auditory Disorders in Children*, Grune and Stratton

Myklebust, H. R. (1964), *The Psychology of Deafness* (2nd edn.), Grune and Stratton

Myklebust, H. R., and Brutten, M. (1953), A study of visual perception of deaf children, *Acta-Otolaryngolica Supplementum*, **105**, 1–126

Newson, E. (1955), The development of line figure discrimination in pre-school children. Ph.D. Thesis, University of Nottingham

Nielsen, H. (1966), *A psychological study of cerebral palsy children*, Munksgaard

O'Bryan, K. G., and Silverman, H. (1972), Learning disabilities—directions for research. Paper presented at the First Annual International Symposium on Learning Problems, Toronto.

Peters, M. L. (1967), The influence of reading methods on spelling, *British Journal of Educational Psychology*, **37**, 47–53

Piaget, J. (1952), *The Origins of Intelligence in Children* (2nd edn.), International Universities Press

Piaget, J., and Inhelder, B. (1956), *The Child's Conception of Space*, Routledge and Kegan Paul

Provins, K. A. (1967), Motor skills, handedness and behaviour, *Australian Journal of Psychology*, **19**, 137–50

Radaker, L. D. (1961), The visual imagery of retarded children and the relationship to memory for word forms, *Exceptional Children*, **27**, 524–30

Rimland, B. (1964), *Infantile autism: the syndrome and its implications for a neural theory of behavior*, Appleton-Century-Crofts

Roach, E. G., and Kephart, N. C. (1966), *The Purdue Perceptual-Motor Survey*, C. E. Merrill

Robbins, M. P. (1966), The Delacato interpretation of neurological organisation, *Reading Research Quarterly*, **1**, 57–78

Robinson, J. S., and Higgins, K. E. (1967), The young child's ability to see a difference between mirror-image forms, *Perceptual and Motor Skills*, **25**, 893–7

Rock, I., and Harris, C. S. (1967) Vision and touch, *Scientific American*, 216 (May), 96–104

Rosen, C. L. (1966), An experimental study of visual perceptual training and reading achievement in first grade, *Perceptual and Motor Skills*, **22**, 979–86

Rosner, J., and Simon, D. P. (1971), The auditory analysis test: an initial report, *Journal of Learning Disabilities*, **4**, 384–92

Rubin, E. Z., and Braun, J. S. (1968), Behavioural and learning disabilities associated with cognitive-motor dysfunction, *Perceptual and Motor Skills*, **26**, 171–80

Salapatek, P. (1968), Visual scanning of geometric figures by the human newborn, *Journal of Comparative and Physiological Psychology*, **66**, 247–58

Sarason, S. B. *et al.* (1969), *Psychological Problems in Mental Deficiency*, Harper and Row

Schonell, F. E. (1956), *Educating Spastic Children*, Oliver and Boyd

Schonell, F. J. (1932), *Essentials in Teaching and Testing Spelling*, Macmillan

Schonell, F. J. (1948), *Backwardness in basic subjects*, Oliver and Boyd

Schopler, E. (1964), *Visual and tactual receptor preference in normal and schizophrenic children*, cited in Lipsitt, L. P. and Spiker C. C. (eds.) (1965), *Advances in Child Development II*, Academic Press

Schubert, J. (1965), Retest scores on intelligence tests as diagnostic indicators, in Loring, J. (ed.), *Teaching the Cerebral Palsied Child*, Spastics Society

Schulman, J. L., Kaspar, J. C., and Thorne, F. M. (1965), *Brain Damage and Behaviour: A Clinical Experimental Study*, Chas. C. Thomas

Shapiro, M. B. (1953), Experimental studies of a perceptual anomaly, III, *Journal of Mental Science*, **99**, 394–409

Silverstein, A. B., and Robinson, H. A. (1956), The representation of orthopedic disability in children's figure drawings, *Journal of Consulting Psychology*, **20**, 333–41

Sisson, L. H. (1967), *The effects of systematic perceptual training upon the cognitive readiness of Head Start children*. Unpublished Thesis, Occidental College, Los Angeles, California

Slater, D. C. (1967), An experiment in visual perception, *Developmental Medicine and Child Neurology*, **9**, 271–3

Sloan, W. (1955), The Lincoln-Oseretsky motor development scale, *Genetic Psychology Monographs*, **51**, 183–252

Smith, I. M. (1964), *Spatial Ability*, London University Press

Sokolov, E. N. (1963), *Perception and the Conditional Reflex,* Macmillan

Sokolov, E. N. (1969), The modeling properties of the nervous system, in Cole, M. and Maltzman, I. (eds.), *A Handbook of Contemporary Soviet Psychology*, Basic Books

Spivack, G., and Levine, M. (1957), The spiral after-effect and reversible figures as measures of brain damage and memory, *Journal of Personality*, **25**, 767–79

Stambak, M. (1951), Le problème du rythme dans le développement de l'enfant et dans les dyslexies d'evolution, *Enfance*, **4**, 481–502

Strauss, A. A., and Kephart, N. C. (1955), *Psychopathology and Education of the Brain Injured Child*, Vol. 2, Grune and Stratton

Strauss, A. A., and Lehtinen, L. E. (1947), *Psychopathology and Education of the Brain Injured Child*, Vol. 1, Grune and Stratton

Symes, C. K. (1971), *Clumsiness and social status in gifted boys*. Diploma in education dissertation: School of Education University of Birmingham

Tansley, A. E. (1967), *Reading and Remedial Reading*, Routledge and Kegan Paul

Thomas, H. (1965), Visual-fixation responses of infants to stimuli of varying complexity, *Child Development, 36,* 629–38

Thurstone, L. L. (1944), *A Factorial Study of Perception*, University of Chicago Press

Tizard, J. P. M., Paine, R. S., and Crothers, B. (1954), Disturbances of sensation in children with hemiplegia, *Journal of the American Medical Association*, **155**, 628–32

Tyson, M. C. (1963), Pilot study of remedial visuo-motor training, *Special Education*, **52**, (4), 27–33.

Vernon, M. D. (1971), *Reading and its Difficulties*, Cambridge University Press

Vygotsky, L. S. (1963), Learning and mental development at school age, in Simon, B. (ed.), *Educational Psychology in the U.S.S.R.*, Routledge and Kegan Paul

Wapner, S. (1968), Some aspects of a research program based on an organismic-developmental approach to cognition: experiments and theory, in Haber, R. N. (ed.), *Contemporary Theory and Research in Visual Perception*, Holt Rinehart and Winston

Ward, J. (1970), The factor structure of the Frostig Developmental Test of Visual Perception, *British Journal of Educational Psychology*, **40**, 65–7

Ward, J. (1971), On the concept of criterion referenced measurement, *British Journal of Educational Psychology*, **40**, 314–23

Wechsler, D. (1949), *Wechsler Intelligence Scale for Children*, Psychological Corporation

Wechsler, D. (1967), *Wechsler Pre-school and Primary Test of Intelligence*, Psychological Corporation

Wechsler, D., and Pignatelli, M. L. (1937), Reversal errors in reading: phenomena of axial rotation, *Journal of Educational Psychology*, **28**, 215–21

Wedell, K. (1960a), Variations in perceptual ability among types of cerebral palsy, *Cerebral Palsy Bulletin*, **2**, 149–57

Wedell, K. (1960b), The visual perception of cerebral palsied children, *Journal of Child Psychology and Psychiatry*, **1**, 217–27

Wedell, K. (1961), Follow-up study of perceptual ability in children with hemiplegia, *Little Clubs Clinic in Developmental Medicine*, **196**, (4), 76–85

Wedell, K. (1964), Some aspects of perceptual-motor development in young children, in Loring, J. (ed.), *Learning Problems of the Cerebral Palsied*, Spastics Society

Wedell, K. (1965), Shape discrimination and shape copying, in Loring, J. (ed.), *Teaching the Cerebral Palsied Child*, Heinemann

Wedell, K. (1968), Perceptual-motor difficulties, *Special Education*, **57** (4), 25–30

Wedell, K. (1970), Diagnosing learning difficulties: a sequential strategy, *Journal of Learning Disabilities*, **3**, 311–17

Wedell, K. (1971), Perceptuo-motor factors, in Keogh, B. (ed.), Early identification of children with potential learning problems, *Journal of Special Education*, **4**, 323–31

Wedell, K., and Horne, I. E. (1969), Some aspects of perceptuo-motor disability in 5½-year-old children, *British Journal of Educational Psychology*, **39**, 174–82

Wedell, K., Newman, C. V., Reid, P., and Bradbury, I. R. (1972), An exploratory study of the relationship between size, constancy and experience of mobility in cerebral palsied children, *Developmental Medicine and Child Neurology*, **14**, 615–20

Wepman, J. M. (1958), *Auditory Discrimination Test: Manual of Directions*, Language Research Associates

Wepman, J. M. (1960), Auditory discrimination, speech and reading, *Elementary School Journal*, **60**, 325–33

Werner, H., and Strauss, A. A. (1941), Pathology of figure-background relation in the child, *Journal of Abnormal and Social Psychology*, **36**, 236–48

White, B. L. (1967), An experimental approach to the effects of experience on early human behaviour, in Hill, J. P. (ed.), *Minnesota Symposia on Child Psychology Volume 1*, University of Minnesota Press

Wood, N. E. (1955), Comparison of right and left hemiplegics in motor skills and intelligence, *Perceptual and Motor Skills*, **9**, 103–6

Woods, G. (1957), *Cerebral Palsy in Childhood*, John Wright

Yule, W. (1967), A short form of the Oseretsky test of motor proficiency, paper read at British Psychological Society Annual Conference

Zaporoghets, A. V. (1965), The development of perception in the pre-school child, in Mussen, P. (ed.), European research in cognitive development, *Monographs of the Society for Research in Child Development*, **30**, No. 2

Zazzo, R. (1960), *Manuel pour l'examen psychologique de l'enfant*, Delachaux and Neistle

Zeigler, H. P., and Leibowitz, H. (1957), Apparent visual size as a function of distance for children and adults, *American Journal of Psychology*, **70**, 106–9

Zinchenko, V. P., and Lomov, B. F. (1960), *The Functions of Hand and Eye Movements in the Process of Perception*, Pergamon

Zucker, J. S. and Stricker, G. (1968), Impulsivity-reflectivity in pre-school head start and middle-class children, *Journal of Learning Disabilities*, **1**, 578–83

Zuk, G. H. (1962), Over attention to moving stimuli as a factor in the distractibility of retarded and brain-injured children, *Training School Bulletin*, **59**, 150–207

Author Index

Subject Index